Revenge, Diaper and Snacks

C. Ellica

Ukiyoto Publishing

All global publishing rights are held by

Ukiyoto Publishing

Published in 2025

Content Copyright © C.Ellica

ISBN 9789370099005

All rights reserved.

No part of this publication may be reproduced, transmitted, or stored in a retrieval system, in any form by any means, electronic, mechanical, photocopying, recording or otherwise, without the prior permission of the publisher.

The moral rights of the author have been asserted.

This is a work of fiction. Names, characters, businesses, places, events, locales, and incidents are either the products of the author's imagination or used in a fictitious manner. Any resemblance to actual persons, living or dead, or actual events is purely coincidental.

This book is sold subject to the condition that it shall not by way of trade or otherwise, be lent, resold, hired out or otherwise circulated, without the publisher's prior consent, in any form of binding or cover other than that in which it is published.

www.ukiyoto.com

To my children, Mathea, Athena and Jea who continue to inspire me to tell stories that matter. And to my friends, family, my mother and the most amazing warrior (Lola) my grandmother who loves the chaotic life of motherhood.

For the audacity to dream and the courage to pursue those dreams.

He was once the most feared man alive—a legendary assassin, ex-navy, and underground kingpin. Betrayed by those he trusted most, he died a villain's death... only to wake up as a plus-size mother of three, a doting wife, and an aspiring writer with a fridge addiction. Revenge might be on her mind, but how can she plot payback when wrangling toddlers and waddling through suburbia is already a full-time battle? Follow the hilarious and chaotic life of a former badass turned vengeful supermom in this action-packed comedy of second chances, sass, and snacks.

Contents

Chapter 1	1
Chapter 2	7
Chapter 3	21
Chapter 4	34
Chapter 5	46
Chapter 6	61
Chapter 7	72
Chapter 8	85
Chapter 9	95
Chapter 10	104
Chapter 11	118
Chapter 12	133
Chapter 13	147
Chapter 14	161
Chapter 15	171
Chapter 16	182
Chapter 17	186
Chapter 18	192
Chapter 19	200
Chapter 20	214
Chapter 21	222
Chapter 22	231
Chapter 23	238

Chapter 24	243
Chapter 25	249
Chapter 26	257
Chapter 27	265
Chapter 28	275
Chapter 29	286
Chapter 30	294
Chapter 31	301
Chapter 32	310
About the Author	*322*

Chapter 1

I am, what you call, the badass of all badasses.

The kind of name that doesn't just echo through alleys—it carves itself into the walls. People didn't whisper my name in fear. No, they choked on it. Their tongues trembled, their spines stiffened, their knees gave out. I wasn't just powerful. I was power. I am Leon Darrow.

My name was a death sentence stamped in blood and sealed in dread. I was the architect behind the global underworld empire, a labyrinth of sin stretching from Tokyo's neon underbelly to the icy veins of Eastern Europe. I didn't just control crime. I defined it.

Before all that?

I was the pride of the US Navy's elite special ops. Black ops, top tier—missions that never existed on paper.

The kind of man they called when things went south and hell needed a chaperone. An assassin once known only by the number of his kills, now known by the world as a legend cloaked in suits worth more than your home.

I had it all—dozens of palatial estates hidden in the corners of the world, a private garage housing hundreds of customized beasts on wheels, five jets named after gods, and women... God, the women. Models who kissed the ground I walked on. Actresses who begged for my name. Even the untouchables—politicians' wives, heiresses, royalty.

All mine. Just a snap of my fingers.

And soldiers? I didn't have men—I had armies.

Trained killers, cyber-spies, seductresses, and mercenaries who would storm heaven if I asked. My word was law.

My law was absolute.

I was untouchable.

Until *Fate* decided to laugh.

Betrayal. Not from an enemy, not from a rival gang.

No, from Alec Darrow. My brother.

My blood.

He was supposed to be the last person I'd ever doubt. My shadow.

My strategist. The one who stood beside me when bullets rained like hellfire.

The boy I protected in schoolyard fights.

The teen who stayed awake guarding my back in Bangkok.

The man who ran half of my empire with precision and loyalty—or so I thought.

I missed the signs. The too-quiet pauses. The shift in tone. The vanishing reports. I had every clue I needed, right under my nose.

But I was too blind, too cocky.

And Alec? He played the long game.

He used *Blacky*. My prized pet.

A European black widow, a rare hybrid genetically enhanced by my personal biochemist. Its venom? Engineered to kill in minutes—unless you had the immunity I injected into my bloodstream over time. But Alec... the bastard waited. He knew just how long the venom would take in me.

He knew my limits.

He studied me.

I found Blacky's Gucci-personalized cage cracked open. Empty. Mocking.

Then came the symptoms.

Headache. Nausea. Burning lungs. My vision tunnelled as I fell to my knees in my office—a fortress of gold, glass, and steel. The empire I built with blood and brilliance was spinning.

That's when I saw him.

Alec Darrow. Standing over me, wearing my Armani suit.

Holding my scotch.

The smirk on his face could've split the earth.

"For someone like you, brother," he said, voice smooth as silk soaked in acid, "you seemed stupid not to notice your little pet's been gone since yesterday."

His words weren't just sharp—they were poison.

And they cut deep.

Every memory. Every sacrifice. Every time I took a bullet for him.

Gone.

"You were never smart, Leon," he continued, his eyes glowing with triumph. "You were just loud, flashy, dangerous. I let you shine while I built the real power behind the curtain."

Then he knelt beside me.

I smelled his cologne. The one I gave him. The one I wore on the night we swore we'd build this empire side by side.

It made me sick.

Outside, the rain poured like judgment from the heavens.

Thick, relentless, cold as the knife twisting in my gut. The storm above mirrored the chaos below—lightning clawed at the sky; thunder rolled like a war drum. But even nature, in all her fury, couldn't compare to the tempest in my chest.

"Then why wait?" I growled through blood. "Why not kill me ten years ago?"

He chuckled—a low, vile sound.

"Because I needed your legend. I needed your name.

I needed Leon Darrow, the assassin king, the underground saint, the myth, to make me legitimate. While you were out spilling blood, I was buying cities.

While you played soldier… I bought the war."

I clenched my teeth so hard my jaw cracked.

My fists curled, trembling. Not in fear.

In rage. In grief.

"Goodbye, brother," he whispered. "Your name, your wealth… everything will be mine. Because you, the great Leon Darrow… were naive."

He kissed my forehead like a priest at a funeral.

And I?

I burned inside. Not from the venom—but from the betrayal. I wasn't afraid to die. I'd danced with death too many times to fear it. But this?

This hurt. This betrayal shattered me.

I felt my vision dim. The world narrows into shadow.

The storm outside still raged, thunder rolling like war drums echoing into oblivion.

If I had one more breath, I would make him bleed.

If I had one more minute, I would rip my empire back from his cowardly hands.

If I had one more second, I would carve that smirk off his smug face and show him what betrayal costs.

But Fate?

Fate didn't grant me that mercy.

So, as my vision turned to black, as my body finally gave in at the age of thirty-five, I let a single thought echo through the last beat of my heart:

This isn't over.
Because men like me?
We don't stay dead for long.

Chapter 2

I woke up.

But not to the familiar hum of my penthouse security system.

Not to the clink of crystal against aged oak as my tumbler welcomed another pour of 50-year-old Yamazaki. Not to the silence that follows a kill.

No.

I woke up to the most infuriating, ear-piercing sound known to man.

A baby. Screaming like the universe had denied it its divine right to a throne.

It was high-pitched, mocking, unrelenting. It clawed at my mind with every wail. Like a vulture picking at the edge of a fresh corpse. It wasn't just noise. It was chaos incarnate.

I hated it. I am Leon Darrow. I do not entertain such mundane, pitiful noises.

In my world, a baby's cry was a liability. A breach of discipline. Noise was death. Noise was weakness. Noise got people killed.

But the more I tried to tune it out, the louder it echoed—like it was coming from inside my skull. Each shriek made my heartbeat stumble—fast, fluttering, fragile.

Too fragile.

And something else... a coldness.

Not the kind that came from silk sheets on a winter night in Tokyo, or the calculated calm before an execution. No. This was a deeper cold.

Primordial. A soul-level kind of wrong.

Like the universe itself was telling me: "You don't belong here."

Light stabbed at my eyes as I forced them open. The room came into view in blurry chaos. Too bright. Too cramped. Too real.

A dull throb shot through my chest. Right in my nipple. Sharp. Persistent. Rhythmic. "What the actual—" Then I felt it. Warm.

Wet. Suckling. A mouth—on me. Not in the way I was used to. I looked down. And what I saw nearly shattered the last threads of my sanity.

A baby. A chubby little thing. Tiny fists gripping my flesh. Latched onto my breast like it was his. Or... hers? Mine? No. No. No. This was wrong. This was impossible.

Gone were the familiar contours of my body—the steel- forged muscle, the battle-hardened scars, the tattooed warnings across my ribs. Gone was the body that could snap necks and silence rooms. In its place were... curves. Full, heavy curves. My chest was soft, generous.

My skin, smooth and pale. My arms—slender. Weak. My hands—delicate.

Feminine.

This wasn't just some twisted dream. I wasn't in a hospital. I wasn't sedated. I wasn't in some cybernetic rebuild after a failed mission. I was in a different body. And not just any body…

A woman's body. A mother's body.

I tried to sit up—but the baby protested, wailing louder, fists flailing.

And that damn pain returned to my chest like a firebrand pressed to flesh. Then, movement. Two figures. Small. Hesitant. Looming just within the blur of my new vision.

Children. Girls.

One—tall, maybe eleven, skinny and fierce-eyed—stood protectively at the foot of the bed, arms crossed, gaze hardened far beyond her years.

The second—perhaps eight—stood clutching a battered teddy bear, eyes wide with both fear and something worse—hope.

They stared at me like I was a dying sun flickering back to life. Like I was their salvation. And then… she spoke. "Mom? Are you… awake?"

Mom? The word sliced deeper than a blade between the ribs. I blinked. "No—no, no, no, no—what the heck is this?"

But the words came out a croak. A breath. A weak rasp with no power behind it. My voice wasn't even mine. It was higher. Softer. Foreign.

What the hell? I looked around again—really looked this time. The room was a disaster. Toys scattered across the dusty floor. Laundry hanging half-folded on chairs and windowsills.

Crumbs and sticky spills on the corner of a cracked table. A bottle of baby formula knocked over on a torn couch. The ceiling fan above creaked like it was hanging on to its last screw.

A place so mundane, so exhausted, it nearly crushed me.

And yet, those eyes... Those eyes.

Three sets, now—because the baby looked up too, milk dribbling from her mouth, innocent and unaware of the cosmic tragedy unfolding.

The older girl stepped closer. "Mom... you were asleep for a long time. We didn't know if you were going to wake up."

Her voice trembled, but her body stood straight. Like she'd been holding this world together with sheer force of will.

The kind of strength you didn't teach. The kind that was forced on you by life.

My heart—this heart—ached. Not from fear. Not from confusion. But from something dangerously close to guilt.

What the hell was happening to me? I tried to pry the baby off, my fingers fumbling.

Her tiny lips refused.

She whimpered, her brows knitting in protest.

And for some reason, some stupid instinct, I stopped. Why? Why didn't I just throw her off? Why didn't I scream, curse the gods, demand a reset of this madness?

Instead… I cradled her closer. I… shushed her. Me. Leon Darrow. The man who turned drug lords into ashes. The man whose name made mercenaries kneel. Now whispering lullabies to a baby girl… I didn't know what it was. Some buried instinct. Some echo of this body's former owner, now fused with my soul.

Or maybe…

Maybe it was fate's cruel joke. To put a killer in the body of a mother… and watch what happens next. The eight-year-old took another cautious step, then leaned against the bedframe, watching me closely. The eldest's arms slowly dropped to her sides. Her lower lip quivered, but her eyes stayed locked on mine, burning with questions. I couldn't answer them.

Hell, I couldn't even answer myself. So, I did the only thing I could. I reached out. I pulled them both in. They hesitated—but only for a heartbeat. Then they collapsed into me, small bodies pressing against my sides, burying their faces into my arms.

But instead… I let them hold me. And for the first time in my life—not as Leon Darrow, the kingpin… The room fell silent but for their soft breaths, and my own racing heart. I should've pulled away. I should've rejected this false world.

But as this unknown woman with trembling limbs and an aching soul...

I whispered the first words I ever meant in silence: "I'm here."

"Thank you, Mommy, for waking up," the middle one whimpered, her tiny voice trembling. I didn't know what it was—something in her tone, in the way her little fingers clutched the hem of my shirt—but it stabbed right through my ribs and straight into the heart I didn't even know this body had.

My chest tightened. Not the way it used to when I got shot. Not the silent dread of an enemy creeping through shadows. This was different. This body remembered something. Something painful. Something that had cried itself into unconsciousness.

"Mom..." the eldest spoke this time, voice barely a whisper. She sat curled up beside me, her limbs warm, twitching, her brows furrowed in concern too heavy for a child. "Why did you cry last night? I heard you cry so hard..."

I blinked.

Cry?

My throat burned, dry and tight. My eyes ached. Swollen. Tired. "I... I don't remember." The words slipped out of my mouth before I could stop them. My voice cracked. Not like a confession. More like a surrender. "Did I cry?"

"Yeah," the middle one said solemnly, crawling closer, balancing on the edge of the mattress like a wobbly kitten. "You cried for hours... after you spilled the milk from your boobies."

Milk? Boobies?

I stared down at the baby still latched to my—my breast. She gurgled contentedly, cheeks plump and rosy, as if she hadn't just hijacked my whole existence.

"Mommy, did you have a bad dream?"

"I think so," I said slowly, nodding at the middle one's question.

"Yes... I did. It was a really, really bad dream."

"See, Maya?" the middle one turned to her older sister, all confidence now. "Mommy had a nightmare because she forgot to brush her teeth last night. That's why she had the cry-dream."

Cry-dream? Tooth brushing?

The girl huffed and went over to the side of the bed. She knelt, rummaged under the mattress, and pulled out—God help me—a small, square piece of bread that looked like it had just emerged from the underworld. It had spots. It had corners. It was... evolving.

So, the eldest one's name was *Maya*? That was a start.

My mind scrambled, trying to piece together anything I could: names, history, context. I had no idea who these children were, or who this body belonged to. I couldn't remember a thing. Not my name. Not my life. Not even what day it was.

But this body? It remembered something. The way it ached. The way it flinched when the baby cried. It wasn't just the screaming that made me want to punch a wall—it was... guilt. A mother's guilt. Like I had done something terribly wrong before I woke up.

Great. So now I was a guilt-ridden, emotionally bankrupt woman with three kids, zero memory, and a body that made me feel like I needed a manual just to walk.

"I don't think you should eat that," I muttered, watching the middle child eye the bread like it was treasure.

"Why?" she blinked.

"Because it's... um... not—"

"Delicious?" she interrupted, dead serious. "But I already ate half of it this morning. I didn't want to share with Maya."

Then, with horrifying confidence, she bolted across the room, the mouldy bread clutched tight in her tiny grubby hand like it was a precious gem. She even hissed at her sister when Maya reached out. "Oh god..." I muttered, slumping back against the pillow. "This is hell. I've died and gone to hell. The demons are children and the currency is expired carbs."

The baby gave a sleepy hiccup and released my breast with a wet pop, sighing like she'd just solved world peace.

I stared at her. She stared back. Her big, trusting eyes blinked once. Then she grabbed my nipple again like it was her personal stress ball.

"Please stop," I whispered to her. "Please don't touch me. I was a man just yesterday. I paid someone to iron my suits. I shot a man in Monaco for chewing too loud. I am not built for this."

"Mom?" Maya said gently.

I turned. Her voice was quiet again. She was holding something out to me. A drawing. Stick figures. Me, apparently, in the centre, with a crown on my head and the three girls around me. Big hearts. Terrible proportions. Absolute chaos.

"You drew this?" I asked, holding it like it was a live grenade.

She nodded. "We thought it might help you feel better. You've been... sad for a long time."

I stared at her. At the drawing. Then back at her.

Me?

Sad? The body was sad. Broken. Empty. But me?

I was Leon Darrow. I didn't do sad.

But my hand reached out anyway. Shaking. I took the drawing. I looked down at it again, then back up.

"Thanks," I said quietly.

Maya smiled. The middle child barrelled back in with suspicious crumbs around her mouth. "See? Told you she'd like it," she beamed. "By the way, Mommy—can we have pancakes today? Not the burnt kind this time. You burned it real bad last week and said a lot of scary words."

I blinked. "Pancakes?"

"I can help cook!" Maya chimed.

"I can help eat!" the middle child shouted proudly.

The baby burped and spit up on my chest.

Perfect. There I was.

Once the most feared man in four continents.

A living legend.

Now being spit on by an infant while two little girls planned a breakfast rebellion.

And the worst part?

I didn't even know their names.

And I didn't sign up for this.

That was the single, consistent thought rattling through my head as I shuffled—no, wobbled—into what I assumed was the kitchen. Baby on my hip. Hair like a haystack. Wearing a shirt that definitely used to be a towel in a previous life.

I was Leon Darrow.

Former assassin. Ghost of the underworld.

I could skin a man with piano wire and vanish into a crowd in Milan without a trace.

But now?

Now, I was walking around in fuzzy bunny slippers, torn extra-large t-shirt and dodging tiny plastic landmines shaped like ponies and kitchen utensils.

"Okay," I muttered to myself. "Pancakes. How hard can it be? Flour. Eggs. Fire. Boom."

The baby gurgled, as if mocking me.

The middle child—still unnamed—was already climbing on the kitchen counter like a deranged squirrel.

"Get down from there!" I barked, then blinked, surprised at how naturally the words came out. "You'll break your neck!"

"No, I won't," she said cheerfully, reaching for something in the top cabinet. "I do this all the time!"

Of course she does. Of course, this household runs on toddler anarchy.

Maya, the eldest, was standing beside me like a small, stern sous-chef. "You need to use the yellow mixing bowl. Not the blue one. The blue one is cursed."

"...Cursed?"

She nodded, completely serious. "Last time we used it, the pancakes tasted like wet socks and the cat threw up on the curtains."

There was no cat in sight.

I didn't ask further.

I found what looked like flour and what definitely smelled like eggs, and began the sacred ritual of pancake-making—without a recipe. Because naturally, this family didn't believe in such things.

Maya handed me the spatula like it was a holy relic. "Don't flip too early," she warned. "Last time you flipped too soon and then you cried in the bathroom."

I blinked. "I did what?"

"You were very emotional, mom."

I didn't know whether to be horrified or impressed.

The baby was now gnawing on my shoulder like a teething piranha. The middle child was covered in something sticky and was shouting, "I'M THE MAPLE QUEEN!" while pouring syrup directly into her mouth.

Oh God. There was batter on the ceiling.

A plastic spoon in my too greasy hair.

Smoke began to rise from the skillet.

Panic surged. The smoke alarm let out a bloodcurdling scream.

What the fuck is happening?

Everyone screamed back—including me.

The baby giggled like a tiny demon. Maya grabbed a dish towel and started flapping it under the alarm like a pro firefighter. The middle one was trying to save the pancake with a Barbie blue doll. I tried to remove the pan from the fire and dropped it. It landed with a sizzling splat and released what could only be described as a smell of regret and tragedy.

I turned slowly to the girls.

"Okay," I said, completely deadpan. "New plan. We eat cereal."

Maya sighed with the world-weariness of a seasoned war general. "You always say that when the kitchen burns."

I stared at her. "How many times have I tried to cook?"

"Too many," she replied flatly.

The middle child, her face sticky and sparkling with syrup, marched proudly to the table and held up her burnt pancake like it was a trophy. "I like it! It's crispy. Like dragon skin!"

The baby chose that moment to fart with such force that it echoed against the kitchen tiles. Then she clapped.

Of course she did.

I stood there in the chaos, hands on my hips—one of which was now mysteriously smeared with jelly—and let out a long breath.

This was it.

This was my life now.

Cereal in cracked bowls. Maple queens. Cursed mixing bowls. Smoke alarms and weirdly emotional pancakes.

And despite the complete domestic nightmare, the sticky floors, and the smell of burnt batter... I didn't hate it.

In fact, a strange warmth settled in my chest.

Maybe it was a hormone imbalance. Maybe this body was forcing me to care. But when the girls sat down at the table, giggling, chewing, pushing a cereal box back and forth like it was the last resource on earth, I didn't feel the usual urge to vanish through a window.

I felt... okay.

Still confused. Still horrified. But okay.

I poured cereal into the fourth bowl and sat down with them.

And I thought, was there any free time for myself? I need to get my bearings. I need to think. But could I even leave them for twenty seconds without burning the whole poor kitchen?

One of the girls—the middle one, maybe soon I'll learn her name—looked up at me and grinned with cereal stuck to her cheeks.

"You're a better mommy today," she said, mouth full.

"Oh yeah?" I raised an eyebrow. "Why is that?"

"You didn't throw the plate and the pan out the window this time."

Touché.

Chapter 3

I needed to get out.

I had no plan, no money, no identity—but every assassin knows when it's time to vanish. I couldn't take the crying, the stickiness, the weird emotional landmines these tiny humans kept throwing at me. It was only a matter of time before someone expected me to do taxes or attend a PTA meeting or a children birthday party.

So, I did what any trained professional would do.

I ran. *Correction:* I tiptoed. Stealth mode activated.

Baby sleeping in the crib. Maya distracted by cartoons about building an apocalypse banker. The middle one—probably chewing on drywall or licking the faucet. Whatever. I had exactly ten seconds of freedom.

I managed to throw on a yellow hoodie, mismatched socks, and shove my new soft, bouncy chest under a jacket that absolutely didn't zip.

Still. Freedom was at the door.

I was just about to unlock it when—

"CATHERINE!"

The voice hit me like a bullet to the kneecap.

I froze. Eyes wide. Who the hell is Catherine?

Then—

Bang bang bang!

The front door shook like it owed someone rent.

And then it opened. I didn't even know it was unlocked.

In barrelled a five feet woman with the energy of a freight train, arms full of reusable bags, a toddler under one armpit, and a gallon of something pink in the other.

"Oh, my gaahd, girl, you ALIVE!"

I blinked.

She blinked back, then squinted suspiciously. "You look like crap. Like, ugh. Did someone die again?"

I didn't know how to respond. I just stared. Like a possum caught in headlights.

She put the toddler down—who immediately began licking the TV—and shoved a bag of what smelled like dried fish into my hands.

"You didn't answer your phone yesterday! Or the day before! I was about to call the police—or the priest—oh wait, I did call the priest but he's out of town. Funeral in London."

She sniffed. "You've got dead face. You been crying again, ha? You want me to slap your depression out? Sayang ang ganda mo, Catherine!"

Wait. Catherine? So… that's this body's name. Of course it is. Catherine. Of all the names in the universe, I get reincarnated into a Catherine. Meanwhile, the woman was already helping herself to a banana from the counter and yelling at my children in Tagalog.

"Hoy! ALIYA bata ka! What did I say about feeding my Ivy weird things?!"

So, the middle child's name was Aliya…

Then a small, suspiciously quiet voice called from the hallway.

"Auntie Jhing-Jhing, she liked it…"

Jhing-Jhing? A Filipina? From her looks and her amazing accent, I think I'm not wrong. I've been in the Philippines twice and I know for sure the woman who barged in like a tornado was a Filipina.

The said woman whirled toward me like a hurricane in pink leggings.

"She gave my daughter—my Ivy—a dry dragonfly. A dragonfly, Catherine. Like it's dried mango or something! And the worst part? Ivy ate it! She didn't even spit it out. What's wrong with your kid?!"

I choked. "She ate it?!"

"YES! Like pulutan! And now she keeps looking for more in the window! She thinks it's a snack!"

There was a loud giggle from behind the couch, and a chubby toddler popped her head up, proudly showing off a wing stuck to her cheek.

"Ivy, NO!" Jhing-Jhing sprinted after her daughter, who squealed and disappeared like a greased piglet behind the furniture.

I stood there, still gripping the bag of dried fish, wondering how my life went from underground bunkers and bulletproof suits to this—dragonfly cuisine and flying toddlers.

Jhing-Jhing popped back up. "Anyway, are you going to the townhall's meeting later? They're talking about trash segregation and free dental checkups and Mr. Axel's rooster again. If that chicken crows at 2am one more time, I'm going to cook it myself."

I opened my mouth to speak but she was already digging through my fridge like she lived here. "Also, tell Maya to stop giving my eldest horror stories about the closet monster. My kid hasn't pooped in three days. She's scared the monster will bite her butt."

"I…" I blinked. "I'll handle it?"

Jhing-Jhing gave me a suspicious squint, then shrugged. "Good. Ay, your face really looks tired, ha? Did you even brush your hair today? No wonder you always cry in the kitchen. And Catherine—please feed your kids actual food. Bread from under the mattress is not a snack."

I nodded slowly. "Thank you, Jhing-Jhing."

Who on earth told her that?

She gave me a loud kiss on the cheek, pinched the baby on her way out, and disappeared with a final, "DRAGONFLY! You really raised a whole witch, Catherine! You need to tell your daughter to stop feeding the neighbourhood insects. I already forgave her for the wet sardines' sandwich last week, but dragonflies? That's TOO MUCH!"

The door slammed.

Silence.

Maya poked her head out from behind the hallway.

"Mommy? Is aunt Jhing-Jhing mad again?"

I collapsed on the couch, tossed the dried fish bag onto the floor, and stared at the ceiling.

"I don't know, Maya. I think the dragonfly made her emotional."

Aliya appeared, licking her fingers. "It was crunchy."

"Aliya!"

She shrugged. "I saved one in the freezer for later."

I gave up.

After Jhing-Jhing left in a whirlwind of toddler screams, fish smell, and judgment, I just stood there, staring at the half-eaten dragonfly wing on the floor.

Oh God.

Why? Why would you let your child eat those inedible bile things?

What the hell was happening to me? Why was I even alive?

This body... this Catherine... was too big, too soft, too heavy. I could barely walk across the room without knocking into something.

The house smelled like old pizza dipped in milk and forgotten wet socks. There were stickers on the ceiling. Too many. How did that even happen?

One of the girls had taped a half-eaten banana to the wall like modern art.

The children were chaotic.

The screams, the cries, the constant MOMMY!

It was too much! I could handle a grenade but this?

This was too much.

The house was a battlefield.

And not the noble kind. Not trenches and rifles. Not smoke and valour.

No.

It was worse.

It was a warzone of wits, wet diapers, glittery unicorn stickers, and boobies.

There were so many boobies. Not sexy ones. Not fun ones. I mean baby bottles, nursing bras, and tiny toddler hands constantly trying to poke mine to check for milk like I was a vending machine.

There were old crumbs in places no crumbs should exist.

I found a slice of apple inside a shoe and a Barbie doll jammed into a peanut butter jar.

There was a sock in the ceiling fan.

And where was the father?

Was there even one?

Had he abandoned ship in the dead of night and left me—Leon Darrow, elite mercenary and proud bachelor—as the last man standing in a sticky pink hell?

I scanned the room like a confused spy on his first mission, crouching low behind a pile of stuffed animals with permanent marker tattoos. Family pictures.

There. On the wall. A man.

Ordinary-looking. Late thirties. Balding at the front with an underwhelming Mustache. He wore a football jersey two sizes too tight and had one of those dad smiles, the kind that said, "I gave up on sleep in 2009 and haven't known peace since."

Probably the father.

I narrowed my eyes.

He looked almost as old as me.

Definitely not athletic. Definitely had a beer tummy too big for my liking. And honestly, that man didn't look like he could fight off a squirrel, much less raise three demon-angel hybrids like the ones now tearing through the hallway yelling something about "Rainbow Warrior Punches."

I moved to the hallway, still on edge, and noticed a pair of adult shoes by the closet door.

Massive. Size twelve at least.

Way too big for my new petite, unfamiliar feet.

In the bathroom, beside three toothbrushes stuck together with something suspiciously gooey, was a razor.

It was huge.

Silver. Shiny. The kind of razor that said, "I may be emotionally unavailable, but at least I groom."

And yet... there was no testosterone in the air. None of that musky, sweaty, Dad-was-just-here aura I would expect from a house with an adult male in it. Just... Tiny bras. Mismatched socks. Half a cup of milk under the bed—HOW? WHY?

And a scratched-up DVD copy of My Little Pony: The Crystal Heart Disaster playing on loop. I walked over to the TV to turn it off. It hissed. Sparked. Refused to die.

Of course.

I turned to find Ivy—the youngest, I guessed—gnawing on the TV remote. Just... peacefully teething on it like it was a grilled cheese sandwich.

She made eye contact.

Pooped her diaper.

Maintained eye contact. "Right," I muttered. "You win."

I backed away slowly.

Then someone threw a pancake at my head.

It hit me square in the temple with a wet slap.

"Aliya!" Maya screamed from the kitchen. "You're not supposed to throw breakfast!"

"I'm feeding her!" Aliya yelled back. "Mommy said if someone looks hungry, you give them food! Mommy looks very hungry today!"

I peeled the pancake off my face.

It smelled like... was that peanut butter and sardines? My sanity was cracking.

Piece by piece. Like a glass of wine in a toddler's grip.

"Okay," I breathed, pinching the bridge of my nose. "Let's... let's all calm down."

Aliya appeared in the doorway, smeared in jam and holding what looked like a taxidermied squirrel.

She held it out like Simba.

"I found a friend!"

"What—where did you get that?"

"The neighbour gave it to me!"

"Why would—"

"She said it used to be a dragonfly but I stepped on it, so now it's a squirrel!"

That was it. That was the moment I blacked out internally.

I sat down.

On the floor.

In a puddle I hoped was apple juice.

And as if summoned by my internal scream, the front door swung open again and Jhing-Jhing, the pretty plus-size Filipina neighbour of legend, marched in like a maternal warlord again.

"Hey I forgot to tell you about Ivy's birthday party on Friday. You coming, yeah?" She had curlers in her hair now, a giant reusable shopping bag in one arm, and a two-year-old Ivy hanging from her hip like a barnacle.

I blinked at her. My mind was frozen.

"CATHERINE!" she boomed. "You coming, right? You can't say no this time."

"I—uh," I started, but she steamrolled me. "I'm—uh—working on it?"

"Good, but you look pale. Are you okay? You look like you got possessed again. You're not having one of your foggy episodes?"

"...Possibly."

"Well," she snorted, "take some fish. I brought tilapia. And don't feed them cereal for dinner again. I'm serious. Your youngest is starting to moo at people. That's not normal."

She turned on her heel, child still attached to her hip like Velcro, and vanished into the chaos like a legend. I sat there. Stunned.

Covered in pancake.

The baby chewing my sock.

My name is Catherine.

I am a mother of three.

Husband probably missing. And I may be in hell.

I need a plan. A way out.

Or at the very least…

A working dishwasher and a drink with alcohol in it.

This woman… this Catherine…

What was her story?

Where was the husband?

I didn't even know the name of the youngest kid.

What was her name?

The baby who kept cooing and trying to eat my hoodie string?

And where the hell am I?

Am I still even in Ireland?

Or did I wake up in some faraway neighbourhood run by feral children and loud Filipino mothers?

Should I ask the children about their mom?

Would that freak them out?

Would they freak me out?

"Mommy," Maya called from the bathroom, "Aliya is using the shampoo as bubble tea again."

"I'm drinking it with a straw!" came Aliya's delighted shout, squirrel lay dead on the kitchen floor.

I bolted from the couch like a man possessed.

My legs were heavy, my balance was off, and I ran into a toy pony on the way, nearly face-planting into the floor.

In the bathroom, it looked like a war had broken out.

Maya stood on a stool, holding a loofah like a weapon.

Aliya sat in the tub, frothing the shampoo into a suspiciously tasty-looking swirl, sipping it with a red straw.

The baby—who was naked, slippery, and somehow covered in toothpaste—was clapping in the corner like she'd summoned the chaos herself.

"Stop! Stop drinking that!" I shouted, trying to grab the straw.

Aliya just looked up at me and grinned. "But it tastes like grapes."

"That's not GRAPE!" I gasped. "It's lavender and regret!"

The baby squealed and dove into the tub, almost taking me with her as she kicked a bottle of conditioner into the toilet.

Maya, dead serious, handed me a towel. "You've lost control of the situation, Mom."

Oh, had I?

Thanks, Maya.

I grabbed the baby—who immediately peed on my leg—and sat on the floor in silent defeat.

My life used to be simple. Guns. Missions. Orders. Silence.

Now?

Now I was wearing a house robe with kittens on it, covered in baby pee and bubbles, staring at three children who kept calling me "Mommy" like it was the most natural thing in the world.

I sighed. "Okay. Everyone out of the tub. Now."

"But I'm not done making soup," Aliya whined, stirring her soap water with a toothbrush.

"Ivy," I said, finally remembering what Jhing-Jhing had yelled, "is that your name? Stop eating that bar of soap. That's not cheese."

Maya raised her brows, "Mom her name isn't Ivy."

Eh? I sure as hell I knitted my brows like caterpillars. "Well…"

"Mom, you name her, how could you forget? She's Jaya."

Oh…Maya, Aliya and now Jaya.

Great.

Jaya blinked at me with big, innocent eyes…then took a bite anyway.

Chapter 4

Later that night…

After an exhausting hour of brushing tangled hair, pulling socks out of the microwave (long story), and convincing Maya that shadows aren't sentient creatures out for revenge, I collapsed onto the living room rug.

The three girls had finally fallen asleep in a pile on the couch, breathing softly like little wolves who'd successfully taken down their prey.

I stared at the ceiling, trying not to cry from confusion.

Who was Catherine? Why was I in her body? Where was I supposed to go from here?

"Should I ask the children about their mother?" I muttered aloud. "This family? Their history? Their address?"

Damn it!

I groaned. "God. Am I even still in Ireland?"

There was no answer. Only the soft snoring of Aliya—who, in her sleep, rolled over and muttered one word:

"Dragonfly…"

I sighed and buried my face into a pillow.

I'm Leon Darrow. Once a shadow in the night. Now apparently... Mother of three.

God help me...

I froze. Oh right.

The internet.

Of course.

The most powerful tool of the modern age.

It had all the answers I needed: where I was, who Catherine was, how I got into her body, and—most importantly—how to escape.

I needed a phone. Or a laptop. A tablet. Anything with Google and enough battery to last longer than my patience.

I stood, with all the grace of a war-torn general, and began rampaging through the living room. There were toys everywhere.

And not just normal toys.

Half-toys. One-armed Barbies.

A Ken head inside a teacup.

A chewed-up remote control that smelled faintly of applesauce.

Into the kitchen I went. More chaos. Stickiness. What looked like spaghetti glued to the ceiling.

Still no phone. I nearly tripped on a tricycle with only two wheels and found a suspicious pile of glitter and LEGOs stacked like a shrine to chaos.

And finally, there it was. Hidden inside a small, pink, broken dollhouse.

A phone. Or… something phone-shaped.

I picked it up like it was cursed. It was covered in dry oatmeal, sticky cereal flakes, and possibly a hint of peanut butter. It didn't even look like it had known a charger in this century. But I'm Leon Darrow.

I've survived gunfire, three cursed bombs in Afghanistan, and the wrath of a vengeful ex-girlfriend.

A cereal-covered phone? Please. I can do this. I began rampaging again, looking for a charger with the desperation of a raccoon on Red Bull. Flipping couch cushions.

Kicking over baskets. Digging through drawers full of unpaired socks, broken crayons, and old takeout menus.

And then I found it. Inside an empty fishbowl. Of course. Because why wouldn't the charger be in a goddamn aquarium?

The cable was a little soggy, and—wait—chewed. I held it up to the light. Bite marks.

Small teeth. Maybe a rat. Or a child. Or a child raised by rats. I didn't want to think about it. I plugged the phone in anyway.

A spark shot out; smell of burnt marshmallows filled the room. The phone screen blinked. Died. Blinked again. It was… trying. Like me. But it wouldn't charge.

I stood up slowly.

Trembling with the weight of defeat and leftover pancake on my socks. There was only one thing to do. Visit the neighbour, Jhing Jhing.

*****

Ten minutes later, I was still at Jhing-Jhing's door, nodding like a polite hostage.

She lived just a few doors away, but it felt like a journey across the Sahara. She opened the door wearing a Hello Kitty robe and mismatched slippers, her hair in an elaborate nest of curlers, a wooden spoon in one hand and a toddler clinging to her leg like a spider monkey.

"Hi Catherine!" she chirped, not even letting me speak. "I was just thinking about you, you know! I told Jun that I dreamed about you last night again, you were a jellyfish and I was a giant shrimp, and we were doing Zumba underwater, tapos—do you Zumba pa ba? You look like you lost weight, or maybe it's just the pyjamas…"

I smiled politely. Nodded.

Did not understand a word.

"Uh… Jhing," I interrupted finally, after ten minutes of shrimp dreams and telenovela spoilers, "do you have… a phone charger I could borrow?"

"Oh! Yes, yes yes. I think Ivy put it in the rice bin. Hold on!" she disappeared into her kitchen like a pink hurricane.

When I finally returned home, triumphant, my phone plugged into the rice-dusted charger, I felt like a soldier bringing fire to the cavemen.

I stared at the charging phone. My hands trembled in anticipation.

Finally, I could make sense of everything.

But then... No face recognition. "What on earth?"

I blinked. Tried again. Still nothing. "Of course," I muttered. "Of course, this woman couldn't afford Face ID."

I looked around the room.

Looked down at myself.

A loose shirt with a stretched neckline, boobs slightly jiggling with each movement, and a pair of over washed pink boxers that had definitely seen better decades.

And don't even get me started on the bra.

I knew Armor. I knew Victoria Secret.

I knew corsets cursed by mad witches.

this bra? It was suffering incarnate. The underwire had been replaced with hope and prayer. One cup sagged. The other was stuffed with a baby sock. I stared at the phone again.

"She couldn't even afford new underwear," I whispered. "What more a phone?"

I collapsed back onto the couch—well, technically a foldable mattress shaped like a donut—while My Little Pony glared at me from the still-looping DVD screen.

I slumped back onto the stained couch, the sagging cushions sighing under my weight like they, too, were exhausted by life.

My back ached. My neck throbbed.

My shoulders felt like I'd carried the weight of three worlds—which, in this case, might have been literal.

The screaming kids, the broken charger, the dragonfly-eating neighbours, and now this damned body that creaked with every breath—it was too much. Every bone in this too-soft, too-slow, too-foreign body screamed in betrayal. Even the air felt heavier, like I was breathing through disappointment.

My knees cracked when I stood.

My spine groaned like it wanted to give up.

"I was a man of war, a man of steel. And now—I'm sweaty, saggy, and someone's mother."

I clenched my fists, resisting the urge to scream as Jaya hurled a Barbie doll straight at my temple and giggled like a tiny gremlin.

The doll bounced off my forehead with an insulting "thwop."

I wanted to throw something. Instead, I looked up at the calendar on the wall.

A red circle marked today.

BB's Bday. 08212024

I squinted.

"Jaya's birthday?" I muttered, remembering the brief scribbles on the notes app earlier. "BB must be baby."

Of course. Jaya. The baby girl.

The one currently trying to eat a crayon in the corner. Maybe it was the password.

Desperation pushed me. My fingers were trembling—not with fear, but with sheer burning rage at the universe.

I typed it in. Jaya's birthday. It took me three tries. The touchscreen was cracked. The phone lagged like it was reconsidering its purpose in life.

But finally— It opened. And I swear, at that moment, it felt like I had just won a bid for a billion-year-old artifact. Not because of the money.

No. This was deeper than wealth.

This was the first thing that had gone right since I woke up in this soggy diaper circus of a household.

I grinned. No—I almost cried. I had power. I had knowledge.

And in ten minutes, that power shattered me. Emails. Messages. Notes. Calendar.

It was all there.

Catherine O'Sullivan. Half Irish, half Korean.

Married to Ray O'Sullivan, a truck driver who worked deliveries to Scotland and came home every weekend.

The man was real. Just not present. The adult shoes. The razor. The unwashed smell of man lingering faintly in the hallway—I wasn't hallucinating.

They had been married for ten years. No living parents. No siblings. Just her and the girls and this dump of a life.

And yes—I was still in Ireland. Galway, to be exact. A sleepy suburb. A forgotten apartment. An exhausted woman trying to keep it together. I flipped through school emails.

Maya was in fifth grade. Smart, according to a teacher's note. Loves cats. Aliya, in third, had been caught feeding dried insects to classmates more than once.

Jaya, the baby, was a walking hurricane in a bib.

Then I found the news. The moment that sliced me in half. A tab open in the browser:

"Leon Darrow Dead: Billionaire Bad Boy Killed by Own Exotic Pet."

I clicked it.

Dozens of headlines followed.

"Tech Empire Mourns the Death of Leon Darrow."
"From Orphan to Oil Tycoon: The Leon Darrow Legacy."
"Greek Supermodel Dorothy Mourns Tragic Death of Lover."

Photos of me in my prime. Suited. Grinning. Powerful. Alive. And a shot of Alec. The bastard! My brother. Standing at my funeral.

Delivering a eulogy with tears I knew were fake. And just like that, I felt it—A black fire twisting in my gut.

He took everything. My company, my properties, my assets, even Dorothy—the woman I had saved from a yacht fire in Santorini. She looked radiant beside Alec now, like she'd never known me. Like I was just a bad dream. "Alec inherits the Darrow Estate after tragic accident," one article read.

He had won. And I?

I was buried in the past, in a grave labelled by my own stupidity.

I had trained that spider myself. Fed it. Pampered it. *"Famous bachelor dies from venom of rare pet spider—authorities unsure if it was accidental."*

My lips curled in silent fury.

They called it accidental? Please.

I knew Alec. I knew how he worked.

Subtle. Precise. Always behind the curtain pulling strings while smiling on stage.

He'd done it. He'd taken everything.

And now I was stuck in the body of a mother of three with saggy breasts and a broken phone charger.

My chest tightened with the weight of unbearable rage.

My hands were trembling again.

Not from grief—this was something hotter.

Darker.

I closed the phone with a snap.

And I screamed. Internally.

Externally, I just stared at the cracked ceiling while Jaya climbed onto my lap and tried to open my mouth with her chubby fingers.

"I need a plan," I whispered. "I need to think."

A silence fell across the room as the TV shifted to static.

Aliya farted audibly in the kitchen. *Just you wait, Alec. Just you wait.*

That night, I didn't sleep. I couldn't.

Not with the weight of rage, regret, and baby drool slowly soaking through my only clean shirt. The kids eventually passed out like knocked-out gremlins.

Jaya had fallen asleep hugging a carrot.

Aliya snored while spooning a hairbrush.

Maya clung to my side like I was still her mother—and not a dead billionaire trapped in Catherine's squishy body.

But I remembered something.

A failsafe. A last card I'd hidden long ago.

Back when I still wore Italian leather and not cat-print pyjama pants from Penneys.

"In case of absolute betrayal," I had told myself, *"Don't rely on digital. Bury it. Hide it like your life depends on it."*

Because maybe it would.

And now it did.

There was a stash.

Somewhere.

Hidden in a cabin I bought under a different name, tucked in a mountain just a few towns away. Inside that cabin was:

One unregistered gun
Two burner phones
Three ATM cards
An international passport under the name "Leonard Hahn"
Several envelopes stuffed with Euros, Dollars, and Yen
And a watch that could access my off-grid account in Switzerland

No one—not even Alec—knew about it.

I could almost hear the man's smug voice now, sitting on my throne, probably wearing my watch, fondling my old life like it was a souvenir.

I was getting it back. But first—

I needed a car.

The Next Morning… I stood outside Jhing-Jhing's door at 7:12 a.m., clutching a squirming baby under one arm and a bag packed with mismatched socks, juice boxes, and a metal spoon (Aliya said it was her weapon).

I knocked. Hard. The door opened almost instantly.

And there she was—Jhing-Jhing.

A plus-sized Filipina goddess of pancakes and unsolicited advice, wrapped in a massive unicorn robe and holding a steaming mug that said "Don't Talk to Me If You're Skinny."

"Oh, my gulay," she gasped, eyes wide. "Catherine?! You're awake?! Praise Jesus and all his backup dancers!"

"I need a car," I said.

She blinked. "A car?"

"Yes. Yours."

Silence.

"Really?" Then she laughed so hard, she nearly choked on her own morning breath. "Oh, ho ho! What happened, you planning to elope with a milkman?"

Maya stepped forward. "Mommy said we're going on an adventure."

"I did," I nodded solemnly.

Aliya added, "She also said something about 'revenge' and 'Swiss accounts' but I don't know what that means."

Jhing-Jhing paused. "Ahhh... sleep deprivation. I remember those days. Okay, fine. You can borrow Tito Eddie's van. But return it, ha? We use that for Sunday karaoke."

Chapter 5

The van smelled like dried shark and old wet clothes. I sat in the driver's seat, straining against the wheel, while Aliya used a jump rope to tie her stuffed duck to the headrest.

Maya acted like my GPS.

"We turn left, right? Then past the big cow statue?"

"I don't know," I muttered. "Does the cow have sunglasses?"

"Yup! That one!"

Baby Jaya shrieked and began slapping her feet on the dashboard.

It took us three hours.

Three hours of nonstop screaming, vomiting (Aliya again), diaper explosions, and me seriously questioning if revenge was still worth it.

But the moment I saw the mountain road curve toward that familiar treeline, something inside me stirred.

Hope. Rage. A flicker of something I hadn't felt since I died. Purpose.

It looked exactly as I remembered—small, gray, with vines creeping up the sides like nature was trying to reclaim it. The lock was rusted, but I had buried a key under a fake rock beside the door.

Aliya stepped on it and screamed, "MOM THERE'S A SPIDER UNDER THE ROCK—Can I pet it? I froze.

"No, hell no!" We stepped inside.

"Mom, is this our cabin?" Maya asked and looked around the dust covered excuse of a cabin.

"It is now."

Aliya groaned, "Did we steal it?"

"Of course not."

"Ah! It's not exciting anymore."

Dust and time had done their worst, but the cabin still stood solid. The couch was torn, the fireplace was filled with twigs, and the floorboards creaked like a horror movie waiting to start.

I moved to the fireplace, crouched down, and pulled a loose brick from behind the andiron. There it was. A metal lockbox, perfectly intact. My hands shook. This was it. The old me. The true me. I opened it.

Inside were:

The black passport, pristine.
A Glock 19, wrapped in a cloth.
Two burner phones, both still working.
Three ATM cards marked with international bank names.
Envelopes fat with money—clean, untouched, free.
And at the bottom, my watch—the biometric key to my Swiss vault. I grinned like a madman. Leon Darrow wasn't gone.

He was just biding his time.

"Mommy," Maya whispered behind me, eyes wide, "Are we… secret agents?"

"Yes," I said.

Aliya whooped. "Can I be a dragon spy?!"

Jaya farted in response.

I clutched the gun, the watch, and the passport.

The world thought I was dead. But now? Now I had kids, chaos, and cold hard cash.

But let the war begin.

We were halfway down the winding road back to town when the golden arches appeared in the distance like a heavenly sign from above. McDonald's. Now, I've eaten caviar flown in from the coast of Spain.

I've dined at Michelin-starred restaurants where the waiter uses tweezers to place a single parsley leaf on your duck confit.

But this? This was war food. And I was a soldier—tired, broke, and mentally unhinged.

I pulled into the drive-thru with the intensity of a fugitive making a drug deal.

"Welcome to McDonald's, can I take your order?"

"Yes. Everything."

"Pardon?"

"I want the greasiest, juiciest, cheapest, most cholesterol-packed feast you've got. Nuggets, burgers, fries, sundaes. I don't care. Throw in Happy Meals. Four of them. I want the toys."

The van smelled like victory and heartburn. I handed a nugget to Maya, who promptly threw it back at me and screamed, "TOO HOT!"

Aliya licked her sundae like a wild animal while Jaya examined every toy for "magical properties."

The silence that followed as they all stuffed their faces was the most peace I'd had in days.

I chewed into a Big Mac, sauce dripping down my borrowed unicorn-print hoodie, and I swear to all the gods of vengeance—

"This is the most disgusting, amazing, chemically satisfying thing I've ever tasted."

I even ordered takeout for Jhing-Jhing and her girls.

A thank-you for the van. And for not reporting me to child services.

*****

We arrived back at the apartment looking like we'd just looted a food truck.

The kids crashed onto the couch, fries in their hair, ketchup on their cheeks, and Happy Meal toys in their socks.

I dumped the bags of food onto the kitchen table and began distributing things like a war general handing out rations.

That's when Aliya pointed at the black case I carried in from the van.

"What's that, Mommy?"

I froze mid-nugget.

Maya peeked over her sister's shoulder.

"It looks like one of those briefcases' spies carry in movies. Is that a toy?"

"Is it a nerf gun?" Aliya squealed, reaching for the handle.

I blocked her with a reflex I didn't even know Catherine's body had. "No touching."

"Is it fake?" Maya asked. "Are you working on a costume or something?"

I sighed, setting the case gently on the top shelf of a cabinet far from their hands. "It's… grown-up stuff."

"Like bills?"

"Yes. Very boring, dangerous bills."

Aliya narrowed her eyes. "You're hiding treasure."

"Of course not," I changed the subject by tossing them more fries.

Later that Night…

Once they passed out from the sugar crash of a century, I sat alone at the kitchen table, phone in hand, notes app open, money still hidden, gun safely locked in the broken breadbox I rigged with a padlock.

I opened a new note.

THE PLAN:

Lose weight. *(This body is dying just from stairs. I will not let my knees betray me like this.)*

Hire a professional cleaning service. *(This place smells like crayons and despair.)*

Buy a car. *(Jhing-Jhing's van sings when it turns left. Like an old woman in pain.)*

New clothes for the kids. (Maya's wearing a shirt with holes and Aliya's underwear has Elsa's face literally peeling off.)

Groceries. *Real groceries. Not just yogurt tubes and expired oatmeal.*

Figure out how to approach Alec without getting murdered. Or arrested. Or both.

Get my name back. *My money. My company. My pride.*

I paused. Added one more.

Keep the kids alive. Somehow.

I leaned back in the chair, arms behind my head, staring at the cracked ceiling above me.

I had been a billionaire, a CEO, a man feared and respected.

Now I was a sticky, exhausted, debt-ridden mother of three, hoarding a Glock in a cupboard next to baby formula.

And for some reason?

I didn't completely hate it.

The Next Morning

I woke up with purpose. I had a plan. I was determined. "Today, I take back control."

4:00 a.m. sharp.

The house was silent.

The kids were still drooling into their pillows, the My Little Pony DVD had stopped looping, and all I could hear was the ticking clock and my cracking knees.

I stood in the middle of the living room in Catherine's—my—old oversized hoodie and mismatched pajama bottoms that read "I run on coffee and chaos."

Step One: Basic exercise.

"Let's go, Leon. You've faced boardroom battles. Hostile takeovers. You can do this."

I dropped to the floor.

One push-up.

Crack. Pop. PAIN.

Jesus! it was painful, how could this woman bear such a heavy task? One push up and it felt like the world itself ceased to exist.

I let out a wheeze that sounded like a tea kettle on its deathbed. Tried a sit-up.

The fat on my stomach folded in on itself like an emotional support blanket.

By the time I attempted a lunge, I lost balance and ended up lying flat on my back, one leg in the air, like a broken wind-up doll.

"This… is not a body. This is a sack of potatoes held together by regret."

I fell asleep on the cold linoleum floor, breathing like a dying animal, vaguely aware of my own feet smelling like chicken nuggets.

*****

"MOMMMMMM!!!"

I jolted awake.

My spine screamed.

My soul screamed.

My eyes barely adjusted to the morning sun filtering through the window blinds like judgemental spotlights.

Maya's voice echoed from the hallway. Then— "She did it again! Mooooomm! Theres' a poooo!!!"

"Oh god."

This was a war against Sparta and diapers. I sat up like a zombie with back pain and hobbled toward the sound of doom.

In the bathroom, Maya stood frozen, toothbrush in hand, pointing like a horrified detective at a puddle of something that definitely wasn't water. "ALIYAAAA!" I croaked. From the kitchen, I heard the clatter of bowls. Aliya popped her head in with a guilty smile and zero shame. "It slipped."

"S-SLIPPED?" Maya cried. "It's ON THE FLOOR! Like a log! How does that even SLIP?!" I turned to her, trying to be the adult here, the authority. "Aliya, we do NOT poop on the floor."

"It was an emergency," she shrugged. "I thought it was a fart. But then it wasn't. So I ran." I leaned against the door frame and nearly wept.

Meanwhile, Jaya, the baby, began screaming in the other room. A shrill cry that said I'm hungry, angry, and possibly teething.

I limped into the kitchen, where Jaya sat in her high chair, yeeting plastic spoons across the room like a tiny warlord.

The toaster was broken. The milk had gone bad. The cereal was stuck together in one giant rock. I tossed it in the sink and dug out the emergency food from yesterday's McDonald's leftovers.

"Here," I said, handing Maya and Aliya semi-warm fries and a microwaved burger split in two. "Breakfast of champions."

Maya stared. "This isn't healthy, mom?"

"Neither is the trauma from this morning," I muttered.

Aliya shoved a fry in her mouth. "This is the best day ever. Mom, you are the best of all the bestttessst in the whole earthhhh."

I rolled my eyes at her and somehow got Maya into her school uniform alive, Aliya into... well, something clean-ish, and braided their hair like a drunken centaur.

It was passable. Kind of.

Backpacks on. Lunchboxes filled with string Doritos, banana, cookies, and a note that said, "Do your best. Love, uh, me."

I kissed them both on the forehead, shocked at how natural it was starting to feel.

Me, the badass of all badasses.

Damn!

Even if my legs were jelly, my hair was frizzing, and my back felt like it'd been stomped by horses.

"Okay girls, time for school. I love you. Don't poop on anything that isn't a toilet."

Maya rolled her eyes. "That's not how normal moms talk."

I opened the front door and watched them walk out toward the bus stop.

Somehow, the sun felt a little warmer.

Then Jaya sneezed directly into my mouth and laughed maniacally.

After getting Maya and Aliya out the door and praying to whatever gods watched over rogue billionaires stuck in mom bodies, I sagged onto the nearest chair with Jaya balanced on my lap like a warm bowling ball.

Her chubby little hands smacked my cheeks like I was some sort of bongo drum.

"Keep it together, Leon. You've handled million-dollar mergers. You are a warrior. You are the most feared assassin. You can handle a baby."

Nope. Her nose was running, her diaper smelled like nuclear fallout, and she kept babbling nonsense like she knew my weakness. Then she threw up on my chest.

"This is fine," I muttered, voice hollow, eyes empty.

I needed help. Not just help—professionals.

So, I cleaned myself the best I could, propped Jaya into a sling that barely fit over these gloriously maternal mammaries, and waddled to Catherine's crusty oatmeal phone. After three different cleaning apps failed to load, I gave up and messaged Jhing-Jhing, the neighbour, who knew everyone and their grandmothers.

Me: "Do you know a cleaner? Urgent. Like... life or death."
Jhing Jhing: *"OMG beshy why? You expecting someone? Date?"*
Me: "No. Mold. Children. Floor poop. Send help."

Within ten minutes she responded with, "Rosita and Sons Cleaning Services incoming. Don't forget to offer snacks. They're allergic to attitude."

When the cleaners arrived—two older women, a teenage boy, and a mop that looked possessed—I nearly cried.

I paid them triple.

Rosita looked me up and down, then at the baby chewing her own sock.

"Oh hija. You look like a broken piñata."

I nearly hugged her.

They got to work, diving into this biohazard of a house like warriors of cleanliness.

Within five hours, the living room had visible floor, the kitchen smelled like bleach instead of despair, and even the toilet sparkled.

I sat with Jaya, who was now licking the TV remote. "We are reborn," I whispered.

She burped in agreement.

Next up: food.

With Maya and Aliya in school and the house no longer resembling a warzone, I dressed Jaya in a fluffy pink jacket and slipped on a blue hoodie over my unwashed hair.

I looked like a tired influencer who gave up halfway through a makeup tutorial.

"Let's go get food, tiny tyrant."

The walk to the grocery store felt like crossing a desert.

Everything ached. My knees, my hips, my soul.

I waddled past mirrored glass and caught my reflection—massive, puffy, and frizzy-haired.

Inside the store, I grabbed a cart and started filling it like a mom possessed. Diapers, baby wipes, milk formula because there was no way I'm going to nurse her again.

My pride couldn't handle another tugging and pulling.
Then Baby food. Fruit that looked healthy.

Frozen pizza and pasta. Snacks I didn't even recognize. Cleaning wipes and more chips Two gallons of milk, boxes of cereals, pancakes and slices of bread.

Jaya started crying mid-aisle. Loud, public, soul-piercing wails. People stared. My back was sweating. My boobs jiggled with every panicked breath. The cart was too full. The baby was too loud.

I was a former billionaire who used to buy $1000 steaks flown in from Kyoto—and now I was chasing a pacifier across the floor like a raccoon. "It's okay, sweetheart," I cooed, trying to remember how human mothers sounded. "You want the apple sauce? Or should I give you, my soul? Either works."

A kind older lady helped me pick up the dropped bottle, and gave me that knowing mom-to-mom look. "First time out alone with the baby?" she smiled.

I nodded mutely, cheeks burning.

Inside, I was screaming.

Leon Darrow, real estate tycoon, humbled by a tiny human and a sticky grocery cart.

After somehow surviving the checkout lane without collapsing or committing a crime, I loaded everything into a borrowed stroller that squeaked with each step home.

By the time we got back, the cleaners were gone, the floor smelled like lemon and dignity, and I could finally sit down.

After googling everything about what to know about babies, I warmed up some baby food, scooped Jaya into my lap, and spoon-fed her while she occasionally swatted my hand away like a diva.

Her wide dark eyes stared at me, like she was memorizing my face.

"You're a handful, kid," I said. "But you're kind of... perfect."

She giggled with food dribbling from her mouth. And for the first time since waking up in this body, something shifted in me.

I didn't feel like a stranger in Catherine's skin. I felt like someone who had a purpose—even if it came with saggy underwear and back rolls. "Okay," I said, standing, determined. "Tomorrow, we start the plan."

To-do list:

Lose weight (or at least be able to sit without grunting)

Hire a nanny (or an exorcist)

Research how to legally reclaim your life if you're trapped in someone else's boobs

Buy a car

Buy clothes for the kids

Burn the clothes Catherine left me

Set Alec on fire (figuratively... probably)

And think of a way not to have sex with the husband when he returns home.

I looked down at Jaya, who was now asleep in my arms. "We'll make it. You, me, your sisters… and this goddamn stretch-marked destiny.

Chapter 6

Dinner that night was the kind of chaos you could sell to reality TV. The kitchen table was practically bending from the weight of the food I'd brought home—burgers, fries, nuggets, fried chicken, mashed potatoes, apple pies, juice boxes in every flavour, and that suspicious McDonald's salad nobody ever eats but always orders to feel better.

Aliya was shoving fries up her nose and Maya was alternating between judgment and awe.

"Mom..." Maya narrowed her eyes. "Where did you get the money for all this? Did you rob a bank?"

I coughed violently, almost choking on a bite of chicken.

"What? No! Of course not!"

"Then how?" Aliya chimed in; her mouth smeared with ketchup. "Did aunt Jhing-Jhing give you money? Did someone die? Are we rich now?"

I panicked. Fast. My brain scrambled for a story, any story, and before I could stop myself—

"I won the lottery!" I blurted out with the enthusiasm of a woman who had no idea how the lottery even worked.

There was silence.

Maya blinked slowly. "You... won the lottery."

I nodded too aggressively. "Yes. It was just a small prize. Like, um, grocery-level lottery. Not the millionaire kind. More like... the kind that lets you buy chicken nuggets and cleaning services without going bankrupt."

Aliya gasped, then yelled toward the ceiling, "Thank you Jesus!"

Maya remained sceptical. "You didn't even play the lottery."

"Did you?" I shot back.

"No."

"Exactly." We locked eyes in an intense mother-daughter standoff while Jaya, sitting in her high chair, smacked a nugget against the tray like a miniature Thor wielding a golden hammer.

Eventually, Maya sighed and let it go. The food was too good to keep questioning the miracle.

Aliya raised her juice box in a toast. "To lottery money!"

"To lies," I muttered under my breath, clinking her drink with a tired smile.

The girls continued eating, bickering over who got the last pie, tossing napkins like grenades, and arguing about who should get to name the invisible unicorn that allegedly now lived in the hallway.

After everyone was bathed, bribed, and bribed again into going to sleep (Maya with extra reading time, Aliya with five more minutes of jumping on the bed, and Jaya with lullabies and a slice of banana), I finally collapsed on the sofa.

"God, this is more tiring than planning an ambush."

But the house was clean. The kids were quiet. And I, Leon-freaking-Darrow, billionaire-assassin- ghost-mother-thing, finally had a moment to breathe. I pulled out the new iPhone I bought earlier—clean, slick, untouched by baby puke and cereal dust. My fingers trembled slightly as I opened the browser.

Search: Leon Darrow news

The results hit like a sledgehammer.

Headline #1: *"Confirmed: Leon Darrow Declared Dead After Spider Bite in Private Estate"*

Headline #2: *"Darrow's Legacy Divided: Brother Alec Takes Full Control of Empire"*

Headline #3: *"EXCLUSIVE: Alec Darrow Marries Supermodel Dorothy Cleanthes in Surprise Greek Island Ceremony"*

My jaw dropped. "What the actual fu—"

Dorothy. My Dorothy. The woman who once called my abs "a sculpture of sin." The woman I dated for two years. The one who cried when I gave her a diamond the size of a quail egg. And Alec married her. Yesterday. In a castle. Wearing my ring. My suit. My villa. My private yacht. My damn woman.

"Fuck!" I threw the phone onto the couch, stood up in rage, forgot how heavy this body was, and promptly sat back down as my knees gave out.

"That rat-faced, inheritance-stealing, smooth-talking tapeworm."

It wasn't even about love. I didn't love Dorothy. Not truly. But she was mine. She was part of my life, my image, my status. And now Alec had paraded her down a beach like some victory lap over my corpse. I leaned forward, seething, feeling rage pool in the soft folds of this unfamiliar body.

My hands clenched into fists. "You want war, Alec? I'll give you war. You took my life. My name. My legacy. You think I'm dead?"

I looked down at my chest—big, soft, and currently smothered in baby spit-up stains—and sighed. "Okay, yes. I'm not exactly threatening right now. But just you wait."

I stood slowly, legs shaking, and grabbed the iPhone.

"Step one: get revenge.

Step two: get hot."

And as Jaya stirred in her crib, farting softly like a tired balloon, I knew I had something he didn't.

A second chance.

He could have my empire. For now. He could take the buildings and the bank accounts. But I had rage, survival skills, and a three-baby army that feared nothing—not even floor poop.

Tomorrow, I will start planning. Because this wasn't just Catherine's body anymore.

This was my war paint.

And I was about to launch Operation: Petty Resurrection.

It was a Friday morning when I woke up with a plan.

The kids were at school.

Jaya was drooling on a piece of crayon like it owed her money. And I? I was a man on a mission. Trapped in a woman's overly sensitive, constantly aching, gravity-loving body—but still a man with purpose.

We needed a car. Not just for errands. Not just for groceries. But because the Bus of Sorrows had tested every ounce of my soul. The last time I rode it, a man sat next to me and started flossing his teeth with a headphone wire while whispering conspiracy theories about pigeons. Never again. I tucked baby Jaya into her stroller, stuffed some emergency snacks *(half a banana and a cold hotdog),* and marched out toward the nearby used car dealership—Frankie's Friendly Autos, which was a lie because there was nothing friendly about it.

The lot was filled with wounded vehicles that looked like they'd seen the apocalypse and chose to retire here. But in the middle, parked with weird pride, was a banana-yellow family van.

And just like that, I knew. That was my chariot.

Out came Old Frank—the same grumpy mechanic who'd been giving me suspicious looks since the last time I asked if the "car fluids" included hair oil.

He rubbed the back of his neck, squinting like I'd just stepped out of a telenovela. "Catherine? You again? You sure you're not possessed?"

I adjusted my hoodie, stood straight despite my lower back threatening mutiny, and cleared my throat.

"Listen here, Frank. I may look like I've just come out of a lasagna coma, but I know a solid ride when I see one."

Frank blinked. "You do?"

"Yes. That—" I pointed like I was in an action film, "—that yellow van. That's a 2007 model, Japanese make. Front-wheel drive. Four-cylinder engine. Probably runs on synthetic oil. Clean lines. Strong bones."

He raised a brow. "It's a… Honda Freed."

"Yes. Honda Freed," I echoed, pretending I hadn't just read the badge on the side. "A real family beast. Spacious, durable. Great for city driving and maternal warfare."

Frank walked around the van slowly, chewing the inside of his cheek.

"Got three kids now, huh?" he muttered. "This ain't your usual type, Catherine. Last year you asked if the Prius could handle a wine fridge."

I coughed. "That was before… enlightenment."

"Hmm," he grunted. "Well, this one's been sitting here a while. Most people don't want a van that looks like SpongeBob's cousin."

"It's sunshine yellow," I corrected. "It screams confidence. Visibility. Safety. If I'm going to be hauling gremlins around town, I want every pedestrian and pigeon to see me coming."

Frank snorted. "You talk like a mechanic now. What's next, you going to tell me the torque ratio?"

I leaned casually against the van, trying not to let my hip give out.

"Torque's not everything, Frank. What matters is suspension integrity, tire grip, and whether the A/C won't make my thighs sweat in July."

He stared at me for a long time. "...You sure you're not possessed?"

"Only by purpose and caffeine."

Of course, we struck a deal.

Cash. No paperwork delays.

I paid using some of the cash I'd hidden years ago in that mountain cabin.

Frank even tossed in a free air freshener—something called "Arctic Breeze" that smelled like frozen mint mixed with church anxiety.

I buckled Jaya into the middle seat. She looked around wide-eyed like she'd just inherited a throne. I adjusted the rearview mirror and whispered to myself:

"We ride at dawn."

But it was 10 a.m.

Next mission: clothing for the children.

I entered the local department store like a confused war veteran. I had no idea what I was doing. Kids' clothes were organized by age, size, gender, possibly zodiac sign—I don't know. The hangers were tiny. The socks were rainbow-colored cotton lies. And the underwear section made me question everything about this world.

I stood in front of a rack of leggings, holding a pair of glittery pink ones and a onesie with a unicorn farting rainbows, when a soft voice said behind me—

"You look like you need help. Or wine."

I turned.

She was maybe mid-thirties, wearing a red cardigan, holding a toddler on one hip and a latte on the other. Her smile was kind, her eyes filled with a mother's understanding of sleep-deprivation and existential dread.

"I'm Mylene," she said, shifting the toddler. "You, okay?"

I nodded quickly. "I just... I have memory problems. And kids. And... I think this onesie might be evil."

She laughed and took the unicorn outfit from me.

"Let me help. How many kids?"

"Three. Girls. All feral."

Mylene took charge like a shopping angel. She asked for sizes, asked what they liked (I guessed glitter and chaos), and somehow managed to assemble a full wardrobe for all three girls in under thirty minutes.

Shoes.

Underwear.

Uniforms. A special "apology" shirt for Maya that read Too Cool to Listen.

I almost cried. "Thank you," I said as we waited in line at the register. "You're a saint."

"You'll return the favour someday. Maybe to someone else. Maybe to me when I lose my mind next week."

She left with a wave and a smile, and I stood there, arms full of bright coloured bags and baby Jaya drooling on a fresh pack of socks.

Few hours of shopping felt like I was in a jungle in the Amazon forest. It was scary as hell.

Now, we drove back with the backseat overflowing with tiny clothes and my heart… heavy.

This body—Catherine's—had struggled so long. Alone. Poor. Tired. Forgotten. I couldn't believe I had once pitied myself for being stuck here.

But now?

I had a reason. And hell, hath no fury like a billionaire trapped in a soft woman's body, driving a second-hand yellow car, and armed with glitter leggings and the desire for revenge.

Driving home, the van hummed like a lazy bumblebee as we cruised through town.

The power steering was a gift from the gods.

The visibility? Divine.

I could see kids crossing the street, confused squirrels, and even judgmental old ladies walking their dogs in sweaters.

As I drove past a KFC's, Jaya pointed and made a sound that vaguely resembled "Mommy!"

"Fine," I sighed. "Let's try this modern poison." I pulled in, ordered enough food to feed a marching band, and absolutely destroyed two cheeseburgers before we even made it to the parking lot exit.

It was greasy, salty, undeniably sinful—and amazing.

Like biting into a memory I never had but missed dearly.

I ordered extras for the girls. Fried chicken, mashed potato, chicken nuggets. Baby Meals. Fries. And a takeout box for Jhing-Jhing and her little minions, because honestly, she deserved it just for dealing with me and my weird energy lately.

Back home, Maya and Aliya ran outside like caffeinated deer when they saw the van. Their eyes widened when I unloaded bags of food like Santa on a cheat day.

"Mom, where'd we get this car?" Maya asked.

"Did someone die and give it to us?" Aliya said, munching on fries.

I laughed. "I won the lottery."

Their eyes popped like cartoon owls.

"Again?"
"Can I buy slime in bulk?"

They barraged me with questions like paparazzi on a scandal, while Jaya smacked ketchup onto the floor like a modern artist.

I smiled through it. Lied like a seasoned politician.

Gave vague answers. Ate another burger. And for the first time since waking up in Catherine's body, I actually felt... capable.

Exhausted, yes. Sweaty in all the wrong places? Absolutely. But capable.

Chapter 7

The next morning, I found myself standing by the window, staring at the early sun like some moody poet waiting for inspiration. My back hurt. My thighs ached. My shoulders? Non-existent—probably melted into the mattress overnight. I needed to do something, anything, before I started growing roots into the couch cushions.

And so, I decided: It's gym time.

But before I could imagine myself sweating on a treadmill like a majestic walrus, I had to deal with one very loud, very sticky toddler.

"Jaya," I muttered as she clung to my leg with a juice box in one hand and a mystery stain already on her shirt, "you're the boss around here, aren't you?"

She answered by burping. Loudly. Then tried to feed me her half-chewed banana like I owed her something.

Yeah. I needed backup.

I made my way across the hall to Jhing-Jhing's unit. She was wearing a glittery robe and hair curlers that defied gravity. The moment she opened the door; she raised an eyebrow like she already knew I was about to ask something insane.

"Oh wow," she said. "Catherine, you look like a couch pillow that's been through the washing machine."

"That's flattering, thank you," I said, dragging my feet inside. "Hey, do you know someone—anyone—who can watch Jaya for, say, three to four hours? Just a few hours. I'll pay handsomely."

Her eyes narrowed suspiciously. "Why? You going somewhere fancy? A date? Running from debt collectors again?"

I rolled my eyes. "I told you; I won a little something in the lottery."

"Define little," she said, crossing her arms.

"Just enough to buy a used van, a few Happy Meals, and an iPhone. Nothing dramatic. I'm not moving to Dubai. Yet."

Jhing-Jhing sighed and rubbed her temple. "Catherine, you're scaring me. Since when do you talk like a mafia wife on vacation?"

I laughed nervously. "Since back pain became a lifestyle."

"Fine, I'll look after Jaya," she said, already reaching for a bag of toys. "I don't trust strangers with that little demon."

"You're a saint."

"I know. You owe me a Starbucks."

"Make it two, a three muffin and five cheese flatbreads."

*****

With Jaya securely in Jhing-Jhing's arms—already being spoon-fed gummy bears like royalty—I changed into what I hoped looked like activewear. The problem was, everything I owned looked like it belonged to a sad potato trying to go hiking.

Still, I managed. I wore leggings. And a baggy hoodie. And sneakers that squeaked when I walked like I was hiding a duck in my shoe.

I strutted outside like I meant business. Inside I was screaming.

"Be strong," I muttered under my breath, passing a group of joggers who looked like models doing a photoshoot. "They don't know you used to bench press your own weight in Vegas. They don't know you're Leon-freaking-Kingsley. You've just been… rebooted."

I arrived at FlexYCore Gym, a modest little place near the bus stop. It smelled like sweat, rubber mats, and protein shakes. A receptionist with an arm tattoo and neon-pink hair smiled at me like I was already about to give up.

"Hi there! First time?"

I nodded. "First time in this… century."

"You'll love it. We have Zumba, CrossFit, spin classes, and our 'Mom & Muscle' program for postnatal recovery!"

Postnatal recovery? I bit my tongue.

"Great. Sign me up for anything that makes me feel like I'm not ninety."

She handed me a waiver, a bottle of water, and pointed me toward the elliptical machine—a torture device disguised as a helpful aunt. I climbed on. Big mistake.

Three minutes in and I was already gasping like a fish in a microwave. My knees cracked. My shoulders ached. Sweat trickled in places I didn't even know could sweat.

A guy next to me, probably half my age, was running like he was late for a Marvel audition. I glared at him.

"Show off," I wheezed.

He smiled politely. "You okay, ma'am?"

"I'm great," I lied. "Just... recalibrating my soul." By the ten-minute mark, I pressed the emergency stop like I was disarming a bomb.

After what felt like an hour-long battle with my own body, I limped back home with a protein smoothie in one hand and a newfound respect for elastic waistbands. My knees were vibrating. My thighs wobbled with betrayal.

Jhing-Jhing greeted me at the door, Jaya asleep in a blanket fort made from couch cushions and goldfish crackers.

"So," she said, smirking. "Find enlightenment at the gym?"

"I found death and rebirth. In leggings."

"Good. You'll need the stamina. Aliya's school is asking for volunteer parents for next week's arts festival."

"Kill me now." We both laughed. Then I sat on the couch, slowly, as if gravity had quadrupled. Jaya stirred and crawled into my lap like a kitten made of syrup and chaos.

I looked around the apartment. The clean space. The soft lighting. The smell of fries still lingering from last night's binge.

And for a moment, just a moment—I didn't feel like Leon in Catherine's body. I felt like someone rebuilding a life from scratch.

Sure, it was messy. Exhausting. Full of juice-box politics and muscle cramps. But it was mine. And it was just beginning.

*****

Three days later, three days of chaos and gym hell-time, I found myself somewhere I never thought I'd be in either of my lives.

A PTA meeting. What am I supposed to do in a PTA meeting? I have never been into one.

It was being held in the elementary school library, decorated with cartoon owls and paper rainbows, and smelled like apple juice and lost dreams. I was wearing my new high-waisted jeans and a polka-dotted blouse Mylene insisted looked "motherly but not ancient." I felt like a contestant in some twisted reality show where the prize was not losing your sanity.

"You're Catherine, right? Maya and Aliya's mom?" a peppy fake-plastic blonde in yellow yoga pants and green shirt said, leaning over the snack table.

"That's me," I said, grabbing a tiny water bottle like it was a shot of tequila.

"I'm Trina. PTA President. We run the fundraisers, coordinate school plays, and take down anyone who doesn't label their kid's lunchboxes."

She smiled sweetly but with the dead-eyed stare of someone who once made a rival mom cry over mismatched cupcakes.

The other moms sat around folding tables, sipping kale smoothies or sugar-free coffee. A guy named Brett (the only dad there) was sitting cross-legged like a yoga guru, talking about compost bins.

"So, Catherine," Trina said. "We'd love it if you could help organize next week's Arts Festival. It's very hands-on. We need someone with energy."

Energy? I almost pulled a hamstring walking in. "Of course! I love glitter," I lied.

She clapped her hands. "Perfect! You're in charge of the kindergarten macaroni sculpture booth." Macaroni. Sculpture. Booth. Whatever it was supposed to mean. I don't care. But of course, I accepted my fate with a nod, while internally screaming.

*****

That weekend, Maya was invited to a playdate with a girl named Harper whose parents owned a three-story house with a trampoline and gluten-free everything.

I arrived with Aliya and Jaya in tow, armed with store-bought brownies I had absolutely passed off as homemade. The other moms were already in athleisure gear, doing light yoga stretches in the living room while sipping kombucha.

"Would you like to join the stretch circle?" one asked.

"I already did Pilates. With Satan. This morning," I said, which was technically true.

Aliya disappeared with the other kids, and I was left doing my best downward dog next to a woman named Skylar who had matching tattoos with her son. "What do you do for self-care?" she asked.

"I stare at a wall and whisper obscenities until bedtime."

Skylar nodded seriously. "Grounding. I like that."

Jaya exploded a juice pouch on the ceiling right then, ending the yoga peace treaty.

That night, with all three girls asleep in a puppy pile on my bed, I sat on the floor with my new iPhone. I typed Alec Darrow into the search bar again. Photos. Articles. Wedding highlights. He looked like a smug toad in his designer tux, arm-in-arm with Dorothy in her lace, diamond-studded gown. They posed like they were gods of Olympus, when all I saw was betrayal wrapped in a bow. I didn't love Dorothy. But she was mine. Or at least, she used to be. Alec took my company, my life, and now my woman too? It wasn't a heartbreak. It was territorial rage. "You want war, Alec? Fine. You messed with the wrong stay-at-home-mom."

I pulled up a list and wrote:

Get fit enough to chase down a bus.

Open a secret account using hidden funds.

Rebuild my alias.

Find connections in Dublin's underworld.

Make Alec sweat.

I added a sixth item.

Potty train Jaya.

Because the true war was still happening in my bathroom.

The next day, while sorting mismatched socks and deciphering Maya's math homework that looked like it required a PhD, there was a knock.

It was Mylene, the angel from the children's clothing store. We exchanged numbers and found that they were the new neighbours who live a few doors away from Jhing Jhing.

"Surprise! I brought coffee and chaos. Also, you looked like you were five seconds from crying when we last met, so I figured I'd check on you."

I blinked.

She was indeed an angel.

"You are terrifyingly good at reading people."

She grinned and stepped inside, already organizing the living room like a whirlwind.

Within ten minutes she had put Jaya down for a nap, fixed Aliya's doll hair, and poured us both black coffees strong enough to awaken my past life.

"You seem different," she said, sitting across from me.

"Different how?"

"Like you're in a weird in-between stage. Like you're figuring out who you are all over again. It's scary. But... I think you're doing great." I stared at her. Then I looked around. The clean house. The new car. The fridge filled with real food. The kids who hugged me without asking why.

Maybe I was doing okay.

*****

The school festival was one of those events where you expect chaos and you still end up underestimating it.

I hadn't even finished buttoning Jaya's onesie before Maya screamed that the pancake stall was going to run out of Nutella. Aliya, on the other hand, insisted she was going to win the "Tumbling Twister" race even though her entire coordination system consisted of falling face-first into carpeted floors. We were late, of course, and my new yellow family van squealed like a dying cat every time I made a turn. But it was ours, and I was oddly proud of it. *Note to self. Buy a new one.*

Because parking was a challenge—especially when a group of PTA moms blocked the entrance like they were the final boss in a video game. I gave my best "mom smile" and waved as if I'd been one of them forever. Thank God I had Jhing Jhing on speed dial. She appeared moments later in a floral blouse that could double as a curtain, dragging her youngest while balancing two Tupperware's of Filipino sweet spaghetti.

"You're late," she whispered, handing me a paper plate.

"I live a chaotic life now," I whispered back, watching Aliya run straight into a trash can.

Maya immediately ditched me for her classmates, Aliya started a turf war over who gets the last pink balloon, and Jaya was happily chewing on a napkin. Mylene waved from across the playground. She was there too—with twins this time. We ended up sitting beside each other in the small parents' tent, sweating under a tarp and watching our kids wreak mild destruction.

And then the Parent Shooting Booth opened. You were supposed to shoot a series of rubber ducks, rotating on a small conveyor, using a toy rifle. The top three parents would win some school-sponsored mug and eternal bragging rights. Aliya dragged me there. "C'mon Mom! Show them! You can do it! You're like, totally a secret agent, right?"

"Of course not. I'm just me." I muttered. I don't even know how to hold a gun anymore with his body? I doubt I can shoot one. But she shoved the plastic rifle into my hands like it was Excalibur and I was the chosen knight. Parents were already laughing, cheering each other on, some hitting one or two targets.

I took a deep breath. Instinct kicked in.

Click. Click. Click. Every duck. Every bullseye. Silence.

I lowered the rifle, blinking. Even I was surprised. Maya screamed. "MOM'S THE BEST!"

Aliya was already halfway through a conspiracy theory involving the CIA and cloned parents. Jaya clapped and immediately fell backward, knocking over a juice box stand. Meanwhile, Jhing Jhing Jhing shouted from the back, "I told you she is possessed! No normal mother does that."

Mylene, sipping from her paper coffee cup, leaned closer to me. "You're seriously going to tell me you don't remember anything about firing a gun?"

"I swear," I laughed, "I was just trying not to pee myself.

This body doesn't hold tension well."

The three of us ended up in a small coffee shop near the school gates afterward, each holding cups of watered-down lattes and plates of leftover festival cake.

We sat on the plastic chairs like old war veterans. Our kids ran circles around us, wild on sugar and adrenaline.

"You know," Jhing Jhing said, pointing her fork at me, "If you tell me right now that you're either an ex-sniper or got swapped by a witch spirit, I'd believe you. Especially with that shampoo commercial hair you suddenly grew this week."

"It's just dry shampoo and luck," I said, laughing, although something inside me tightened.

For the first time, I felt like I was fitting in.

Like maybe—just maybe—there was something about this life I could learn to like.

That's when I saw it. A sleek black limo.

Just behind the glass, parked in front of the florist's shop across the street. It was unmistakable. Long, glossy, polished, the kind of vehicle you don't forget when you've ridden in it a hundred times to boardroom meetings and red-carpet events.

And inside?

Alec.

In my old Armani suit.

Dorothy. Her head on his shoulder. Laughing. Then kissing. My brother. My woman. The two people who once swore I was irreplaceable now driving around in the same life I had built. The one I lost.

Mylene and Jhing Jhing were still talking, but I couldn't hear them. My ears rang. My latte was ice cold in my hand. My chest—Catherine's chest—tightened painfully.

I didn't even love Dorothy anymore.

Not really. But watching her smile at Alec like he was her world?

Like I never existed?

It was like watching my past die a second time. I clenched the paper cup until it buckled in my grip.

Jaya tugged on my shirt, looking up with round curious eyes. "Mommy, why angry?"

I blinked, forcing a smile. "No, baby. I'm okay."

But I wasn't.

This wasn't over.

Not by a long shot.

I am going to f*ck the hell out of you Alec.

I swear to all the gods of diapers and breasts.

Chapter 8

The next few days passed like a blur—one long, tangled braid of minor victories and barely-contained chaos.

It started on a Thursday morning, just after I'd convinced Jaya not to eat a crayon and Aliya not to wear socks over her shoes "for fashion." The phone rang. Not my new iPhone—this was Catherine's old, cereal-caked phone that I'd kept charged out of sheer paranoia.

The caller ID read: Ray.

Right. *The husband.*

I hesitated for a moment, thumb hovering over the screen. My heart thudded—was he coming home? Was I supposed to act like a wife? What if he kissed me? Touched me? Tried to... cuddle? I wasn't ready to be in bed with anyone while still figuring out how bras worked in this body without dislocating something.

I took a breath, hit answer, and tried to sound as normal as possible. "Hello?"

"Hey Cath. It's me."

His voice was hoarse. Tired. With the distinct background noise of rumbling engines and wind. "Hi Ray," I replied, my tone deliberately neutral. "I'm not going to make it home this weekend," he said. "Took a double shift. Derek—my buddy—he... he died. Car crash. Driver fell asleep on the M9."

I blinked.

"Oh. I—I'm sorry, Ray. That's terrible."

He exhaled. "Yeah. His wife's a wreck. I figured I'll cover for him. Extra money doesn't hurt either."

"No, no, of course. That's the right thing to do," I said, all while thinking: Thank every divine being out there. The last thing I needed was a grieving husband coming home expecting comfort from a woman whose soul had done a complete 180.

After the call ended, I stared at the ceiling in relief. I couldn't explain it, but being alone with the kids was somehow easier than pretending to be someone's wife. For now.

The weekend came faster than I expected. The kids were up at 6 a.m., screaming about waffles. Jaya had somehow managed to draw on the wall with what I hoped was chocolate. And Maya had cut her bangs again—short, uneven, and slightly psychotic-looking.

Despite the madness, I felt... lighter.

Maybe it was the fact that I'd finally figured out how to braid Aliya's hair without tying her ears into it. Or maybe it was because I was finally able to jog three whole minutes without seeing my ancestors. I had even managed to lose half a pound.

Half a pound! It didn't seem like much, but in this body, it felt like winning a damn Olympic medal. I flexed in the mirror, grinning like an idiot. The guilt that once lingered in this flesh—Catherine's sorrow, exhaustion, resentment—wasn't gone. But it was changing. Like maybe, just maybe, I could give her some peace by becoming someone who fought for her kids.

For herself. I treated myself to something cathartic: checking my Swiss bank account.

I had to access it through layers of encryption, codes, and a security question about my first pet that only I would know (Cherry, a spider monkey I kept for a month in college—long story).

The balance blinked on the screen: €58.3 million. I grinned. Time to make life very comfortable. I quickly transferred a modest portion—€25,000—to a new local account under a fresh alias. Enough to make things smooth without raising questions. I wasn't here to make headlines yet. I just needed to survive and rebuild. With money came options.

First, shopping. I strapped Jaya in the baby seat, bribed Maya and Aliya with promises of pancakes, and loaded everyone into the yellow family van. I still couldn't drive it without the windshield wipers going off randomly, but I'd learned to ignore them like an extra personality. We went on a full spree.

Kitchenware: pans that didn't look like medieval weapons, a rice cooker, a full set of cutleries, and enough Tupperware to make me feel like a real adult. And spoons, my gods, the spoons, I've been hearing Jhing Jhing going on and on about spoons missing all the time.

I swear I've checked the spoon in the cabinet and there I found three spoons, very old looking plastic forks and two sets of chopsticks. That was all. The cabinet was almost empty. Pity but for now, this Catherine was lucky. She has me. She can buy all the spoons in the world.

Clothing: school uniforms, pink dresses, shoes, and more pink dresses, books and pencils, socks without holes, rain jackets, tiny boots, and backpacks with sparkles and unicorns. I let them pick what they wanted, and it cost a fortune, but their smiles? Worth every damn cent.

Toys: too many, honestly. But Jaya giggled for the first time when I gave her a stuffed octopus, and Aliya was convinced her robot cat had "powers." And Maya? The beautiful girl that glared at me when I spent two thousand pounds buying her new iPad, Laptop and a new iWatch for myself. It was all worth it.

Then came my things: rubber shoes that actually fit, dozens of shirts, and by gods, some decent undies and compression leggings (which are Satan's corset), and one dozen hoodies that declared "World's Okayest Mom."

Perfect.

Later that night, back at the apartment, the girls helped me unpack the groceries and gadgets. Jaya sat on the countertop like a squishy boss baby while I cooked spaghetti with real ingredients for the first time.

The smell filled the apartment. The laughter, too.

Maya played music on her new tablet. Aliya performed an impromptu dance while Jaya smacked a spoon against her bowl like a war drum. I stood there, stirring sauce, watching them, and thought: This… this isn't so bad.

Later that evening, after all three had fallen asleep, I hired a part-time maid. A kind Romanian woman named Petra who'd clean twice a week and didn't ask questions beyond "Which cleaning solution do you prefer?" Bless her.

I collapsed on the couch with sore feet and a full heart.

The body was changing. I was changing. And for the first time, I wasn't just a rich man in a woman's life—I was becoming someone these children could rely on. I was building something.

Something real. And tomorrow? Tomorrow I'd run four minutes instead of three. And maybe—just maybe—I'd win another half-pound back from the grave. It started innocently enough. Or so I thought.

The morning after our shopping spree and victory spaghetti night, I woke up to the sound of Jaya babbling to herself in her crib and Maya whispering "We're out of milk again…" like a tiny, caffeine-deprived adult. I had one goal that day: survive the parent-teacher meeting at Maya and Aliya's school, then sneak in a workout.

It sounded simple on paper.

Reality check: It was not.

First came the school disaster. I walked into the meeting with Jaya strapped to my chest in a baby sling, a half-eaten granola bar in one hand, and my hoodie inside-out. There were at least thirty other parents. All of them looked…fresh. Composed. Lipstick-ed. There was one dad with a man bun and a tailored blazer that made me feel like a war refugee.

Aliya's teacher started with a presentation. Maya's teacher passed around feedback forms. Jaya started chewing on my hair. Meanwhile, I tried to look like I wasn't about to faint from the smell of someone's lavender-scented cardigan beside me.

Then I heard it.

"Mommy! Mommy, Maya says you were an assassin!"

Aliya's voice echoed across the room. Heads turned. The woman next to me blinked. Her child gasped.

I smiled like an escaped convict. "Haha, kids and their imaginations."

"Maya said you shot ALL the bulls-eyes at the festival. Even the dads couldn't do it!" Aliya added, pointing with a bright red crayon.

A man in the back muttered, "Is she ex-special forces?"

Another parent whispered, "That explains the calves."

I pulled my hood up over my head and laughed nervously. "I'm just… you know. Gifted at foam darts."

Thankfully, the teachers steered the conversation back toward curriculum and reading levels. I practically sprinted out of there the moment it ended, cheeks burning, Jaya chewing my hoodie string like it was a lollipop.

Then came the gym.

I had exactly two hours to kill before pickup and I wanted—needed—to sweat. My body had finally begun accepting movement. I could jog four minutes without seeing the spirit realm. I was determined.

I walked into the local fitness centre called "Iron Den." Red flags? Everywhere. But at least it was different from the last gym.

The man behind the counter was a tank. No neck, full beard, biceps like over-inflated balloons. Tattoos. Skull rings. Dog tags. And a nametag that said, in all seriousness: "BLAZE."

"First time here?" he asked with a grin that somehow reached his deltoids.

"Yeah. Just trying to… get back in shape," I muttered, adjusting my sports bra for the twentieth time.

"Gotcha. I'll give you a private intro session," he said, too friendly. "You'll love my style. Old Navy bootcamp mixed with motherly motivation. For my ladies, I call it: 'MILF Mode.'"

He winked.

I blinked. MILF MODE? "Right. Sure. Let's MILF," I muttered sarcastically.

He started me off on basic warm-ups. All fine. Then squats. Lunges. Planks. Then he "adjusted" my back posture by pressing down right between my shoulders—aka boob adjacent. Twice. I warned him with a look.

He chuckled. "I get handsy when I help. Part of the package."

"Hands off the package, Blaze," I gritted.

Then came the final straw.

"Let's try some punching drills," he said, tossing me a pair of gloves. "Imagine you're hitting your ex, or a bad boss. Anyone who wronged you."

That list was long. He held up the pad. "Now hit me like you mean it."

I did. CRACK. Blaze flew backward. Like, actually flew. The pad slammed into his chest and knocked him clean off his feet. He landed on the mat with a grunt, blinking up at the ceiling in absolute shock.

The entire gym went silent. A teenager on a treadmill gasped. A woman lifting dumbbells whispered, "She's the MILF Terminator."

I dropped my gloves, staring at my hand. "What the hell...?"

Blaze groaned. "Ma'am... are you... military police?"

"No," I said, shocked, then added, "I'm just really, really pissed off."

He gave me a thumbs up from the floor. "Respect."

By the time I got home, Maya and Aliya had already learned about my gym knockout from the neighbour's kid who posted it online. It got seventy-two likes in one hour.

When I opened the door, Maya looked up from her cereal and asked, "Mom... are you in witness protection?"

Aliya added, "Are you John Wick?"

I sighed, sat down, and tried to act casual. "I'm just your mom. Who shops for Tupperware and occasionally punches a Navy veteran across the gym."

Later that night, after the chaos calmed, I got a text from Jhing Jhing: *"We saw the video. Blaze is telling people you're the 'Iron Mama.' Should I start selling shirts?"*

Mylene replied in the group chat: *"Only if she punches someone at the next PTA meeting too."*

I laughed until I nearly choked on my tea. Jaya giggled in her high chair, tossing Cheerios like confetti. And for the first time in a long while, I realized something deep and weirdly comforting: I may not know who I am anymore. But I'm not weak. And I'm definitely not done. Tomorrow? Gym again.

But this time, Blaze wears padding.

Five months had passed since I'd woken up in this body—a stranger's skin, a different name, a life that had never been mine… yet now, every crack of it bore my fingerprints.

The kids were finally in a rhythm—Maya learning chess at school, Aliya hosting tea parties for ants in the garden, and little Jaya now waddling around like a gremlin with a hunger for peanut butter and chaos.

Ray, the legally-binding husband I never asked for, still dropped by once a week—reeking of factory grease and emotional constipation.

He was always tired.

Always collapsing on the couch with a limp "Hey babe," before falling asleep like a corpse.

No kisses. No questions. No suspicions.

Perfect.

Because every second he snored, I was planning.

Chapter 9

It was a Tuesday when I made the decision.

I fed the kids, cleaned vomit off the rug (again), folded laundry, reattached a Barbie head, and then—when the house finally stilled into silence—I pulled out the burning phone.

No one else knew it existed. It had been hidden in the false bottom of the toolbox in the garage, beneath a bag of rusted screws and leftover IKEA nails. Its screen glowed with a faint orange light when I powered it on. Most would mistake it for a glorified paperweight, but it was a relic from a former life.

The names inside this phone could destroy governments. Or start wars.

Tonight, I was doing both. I scrolled through the encrypted contact list, heartbeat steady. There it was:

Fort One – Secure Line

I dialled. The line rang. Once. Twice. Then a click.

No voice. Just static.

I whispered, *"The bees were yellow and it flew backward and screamed at midnight."*

Silence… then a grunt. A breath.

"…What the hell?" a man's voice barked, gruff and thick with disbelief. "Say that again."

"The bees were yellow and it flew backward and screamed at midnight. It's me."

"You're dead," he growled. "Leon's dead."

I smiled; my voice lower. "That's what they want you to think. But Leon trusted me with the contingency plan. I'm his girl."

There was a long pause. "…Bullshit."

I chuckled. "Then tell me who killed Lou Kitsuh in China."

"Lou—Kitsuh—" he gasped. "Leon shot him through a washing machine while chewing mint gum."

"Exactly," I said coldly. "Now shut up and listen. I need access to Dublin's underground. I want eyes on Alec. He's taking over the next shipment from the Tokyo Syndicate, and I want it to fail."

"…You're starting a gang war?"

"No. I'm starting a reckoning."

His breath hitched. "Who the hell are you?"

"I told you," I said, leaning back against the kitchen tiles, the glow from the stovetop clock blinking 12:03 a.m.

"I'm Leon's girl."

Joe Smith—though no one really believed that was his real name—was an Irish ex-mercenary, ex-fixer, and once my clean-up guy in Europe. When I told him I wanted information on Alec, he laughed, cursed, and promised to get back to me within a week.

I didn't wait.

Every night, while Ray snored and the kids dreamed of candy kingdoms and singing sheep, I was on encrypted lines. I used my dormant accounts to trace old suppliers. I bought burner phones. I posed as Helena Shaw—one of my old aliases—and started paying off small-time runners for info.

And Dublin?

Dublin was messy.

The Irish-Japanese alliance I had once maintained was fragile. One wrong move, one delayed shipment, one misdelivered box, and it would fracture into blood and betrayal. Alec—so smug in his suits and ties—had taken over after my "death," thinking the throne was his.

But he didn't know the language of shadows. He didn't understand how a whisper in the right ear could ignite a massacre. I had already ordered a forged manifest swap. If the shipment for the next meeting carried fake gold instead of weapons, the Yakuza would erupt.

And I would be watching with popcorn from afar.

Joe eventually called again.

"Package intercepted," he said. "Shipment was a decoy. You were right—Alec is panicking. He's blaming the Irish contacts."

"Good," I whispered, staring out the window while sipping my fake wine in my fake living room in my fake body.

"And girl?" Joe asked quietly. "What do I call you now?"

I smiled. "Call me Black Widow."

The next morning, Aliya spilled apple juice on her school project, Maya cried because her shoelaces snapped, and Jaya shoved spaghetti into her ears and nose. Of course, I lose my sanity…again.

Ray tried to ask if I wanted to go to his cousin's wedding.

I said, "If I go, there will be no bride left for dessert."

He blinked, nodded slowly, and grabbed his keys. He was pathetic.

By day, I was the stressed-out, oversized mother in red leggings and baby stains.

By night, I was Black Widow—the shadow walking behind Alec's every move. And soon? He'd fall. But not yet. Not all at once.

Slow. Surgical. Unforgiving.

By the end of the month, Ray sat me down in the living room, wearing his best serious face — which still somehow looked like a confused potato — and said, "I'll be gone for about three months. My long-lost cousin from Alaska just found me. He owns a shark boat. You know. Like shark hunting. Or something with fish."

I blinked. "A shark boat?"

"Yeah. Like Deadliest Catch, but with more sharks."

I stared at him for ten full seconds.

"Okay," I said.

He waited, possibly for a kiss goodbye. I gave him a dry smile and patted him on the shoulder like he was a UPS guy dropping off expired milk.

Good riddance.

I didn't care if he was going to Alaska, Mars, or the mouth of a Kraken. I just couldn't have him in the apartment anymore. Not when the very scent of his cologne made my murder button twitch. The mere kiss he gave me on the cheek the other day had made me scream internally so loud that I had to bury my head in a wet laundry basket to muffle the sound.

I am Death himself, I thought.

And this man has the nerve to kiss me with breath that smells like expired salted cornflakes and broken dreams?

A few days later, the gods of chaos outdid themselves.

Maya came out of the bathroom looking like she had seen the abyss.

I was scared. Not by her but to her pink Peppa pig panties.

"MOMMY," she hissed like a dying cat. "There's BLOOD. IN. MY. PANTIES. Am I going to die?"

Aliya gasped. Jaya screamed in unison. I stared at Maya, her hands out like she'd touched something radioactive. I tried to recall the protocol.

Fuck! What should I do now?

Blood? Panties? I am Leon Darrow! I don't deal with Peppa pig panties.

Wait. Did I even buy pads? God, what should I do? I don't know anything about periods. How should I know? I'm an assassin-billionaire-boss for fuck's sake.

Did I have any idea how to explain this without sounding like a biology textbook wrapped in trauma?

What should I do again about tampons?

Damn it! This was way harder than making a bomb. Thank the heavens Mylene arrived like an angel with chocolate, heating pads, and the calm wisdom of a woman who has birthed twins during a typhoon.

She sat Maya down, patted her head, gave her a warm hug, and said, "Welcome to womanhood, sweetheart. You're going to cry about cheese, pink potatoes and hate boys for the rest of your life."

Aliya clapped in excitement. Jaya clapped too, probably because everyone else did.

I sank into the couch and mouthed, help me to Mylene. She winked.

Then the day after, I bought a new car. Not just any car. A white SUV so huge that people mistook me for a diplomatic envoy. The thing purred like a beast, had massage seats, hidden compartments, and AI voice controls that responded to my old code name: Widow.

Ray saw it before he left.

"You renting that?"

"Yep," I said, flipping pancakes and lying like a boss. "Just for a few days."

He nodded, then asked if it had seat-warmers.

I said, "Only for people with a soul."

He didn't get the joke.

That next night, when the kids were asleep—Maya passed out with a heat pad, Aliya snoring under six blankets, and Jaya holding an empty peanut butter jar like a teddy bear—I went downstairs. To the garage. To my war room. What had once been a dusty room with broken shelves and suspicious spider kingdoms had now become something out of a Jason Bourne wet dream.

The walls were lined with encrypted servers. A biometric scanner unlocked a hidden floor hatch that led down into a basement that technically didn't exist on any property map.

High-tech military-grade systems were installed wall to wall.

The air inside hummed with electricity and silent vendettas. Multiple curved monitors glowed with blueprints, maps, and security feeds. And on the centre screen?

Alec's Mansion. No. It was one of my mansions. Thanks to Joe, my ex-mercenary bestie, the entire system was now my playground.

He'd snuck in under the guise of "private security upgrade" and installed a shadow surveillance network routed directly to my laptop. I could see: Every room. Every camera angle. Every time Alec scratched his overpriced hairline and pink lip gloss. Even Dorothy feeding the cat like she hadn't just married my enemy. My brother.

I opened the secure comm line.

"Joe," I said.

"Widow," he replied, sipping something that looked suspiciously alcoholic. "You watching your ex-boo make out with a blonde airhead again?"

"Of course not," I lied, zooming in on Alec as he adjusted his Rolex.

"I'm sending you names," I continued. "Contact my lawyer. The one in Geneva. The property in Texas and Greece? I want them liquidated. All proceeds rerouted through chain dummy corps, bounced through Prague, Paria, Estonia, and then to the underground account in Cayman under alias WIDOWBLOOD."

Joe whistled. "Even the CIA can't trace that web."

"I know," I said, tapping a red key that encrypted all visuals. "That's the point."

He paused. "You know this isn't just petty revenge, right? You're starting to rebuild the whole network."

"I am," I said calmly. "And I'm going to do it with three kids, a part-time maid, and a uterus that won't stop cramping."

As I stared at the mansion's glowing outlines, I felt something inside me shift. This body, once heavy with shame and resentment, now buzzed with quiet power. I was not just surviving. I was transforming. The suburban chaos of motherhood had sharpened me. The betrayal had fuelled me. And now?

The clock was ticking.

Alec wouldn't see the storm coming.

Not until it was already too late.

Chapter 10

It began on a Wednesday.

The kind of Wednesday that smells like betrayal and stale espresso.

Alec woke to the sound of his phone exploding with notifications. Messages. Missed calls. Emails flagged in red. His assistant was screaming through the intercom in five languages, trying to explain the unexplainable.

"Sir, the Texas ranch is gone. We tried to access it yesterday and—"

"Gone?" he barked, shoving away his silk sheets. "What do you mean gone?!"

"It's sold. Entirely liquidated. And the Greece villa too. The sale went through three ghost lawyers in thirty-six hours and was routed through—well, sir, no one can trace it."

Alec rubbed his eyes, tension digging into his temples. "What about the Tokyo shipment?"

"Missing," she whispered. "Yakuza are furious."

He was panicking. He was on his feet in minutes, pacing through his high-rise office barefoot, teeth gritted. "Where the hell is Leon's drive?" he hissed. That's when the rumours began. First, it was a whisper.

Then a blog post. Then a full-blown news segment.

"ALLEGATIONS SWIRL: Alec Darrow Involved in Brother Leon's Death?"

Images of Alec and Leon appeared on-screen — all smiles, all lies.

"Sources close to the Darrow family reveal deep tension between the two brothers shortly before Leon's untimely passing..."

Dorothy stood at the kitchen island, sipping her oat milk smoothie like none of this concerned her.

She blinked at him. "Are you seriously yelling at the TV?"

Alec turned, red-faced and drenched in sweat.

"This is your fault!" he barked. "You and your 'stay out of business' attitude!"

She scoffed, placed her smoothie down, and crossed her arms. "My fault? I didn't ask to marry a man who trades guns and hides money in fake churches!"

He grabbed her wrist too tightly.

Dorothy gasped. "Let go of me."

He did — too quickly, almost as if he didn't recognize himself. She stumbled back, cradling her hand. Her eyes narrowed. This was not the man she thought she married. Or maybe it was, and she was just now seeing it.

"You're falling apart," she muttered.

Meanwhile, in the Kitchen of Chaos

I stood in my kitchen, still in mismatched yellow-green socks, one eyebrow pencil applied and the other forgotten. My hair was in a pineapple bun. Maya was arguing with Aliya about glitter slime and Roblox, Jaya was pretending to be a dinosaur with a ladle, and in the middle of all that—

I was laughing. Laughing so hard I nearly fell off the counter stool.

Why? Because on my tablet, the news played louder and louder.

"Alec Darrow implicated in potential financial fraud, Japanese underworld retaliation pending—"

I picked up a single stalk of broccoli, bit into it like it was a victory drumstick, and chewed slowly. With class. No chocolate.

Not anymore. I was on a diet.

Lost twenty-five pounds and counting. I could run now. Lift groceries without weeping. Even survive leg day.

More importantly, I could still destroy men in the dark with a whispered word.

The Underground Effect

Joe Smith had done his job well. He didn't just sell the properties — he stirred the pot.

The Tokyo shipment was deliberately rerouted to a dock owned by Alec's rival. The Yakuza viewed it as a territorial insult.

Internal documents, edited with pristine precision, revealed inconsistencies in Alec's communication with Leon months before his death. The trail led nowhere. But the damage?

Everywhere. One of Alec's trusted men, Viktor — once Leon's bodyguard — disappeared with half a million in gold bonds and leaked photos of Alec and a military-grade supplier in Argentina.

Whispers turned into flames. Flames turned into headlines.

*****

Back in My World Aliya spilled cereal on the new leather car seats. I didn't care. I am happy. I smiled. A victorious smile.

Maya couldn't find her favourite rainbow Taylor Swift hoodie. I didn't care where it was or why she was screaming at her tablet.

Jaya refused to wear pants and watched Cocomelon lane for hours.

The maid almost quit because she found a stuffed dead raccoon in the laundry pile.

"Mom," Maya asked while I chopped cucumbers with surgical precision, "why are you so happy this week?"

I smiled. "Because justice is like broccoli."

She blinked. "What?"

"Underrated," I said, stabbing a cherry tomato. "And when done right, it makes people cry."

I tucked Jaya under one arm, wiped Aliya's sticky hands, and handed Maya a heating pad for her cramps.

Then I returned to my secret laptop, hidden inside the cereal cabinet behind three fake boxes of cereals. The screen showed a high-res feed of Alec, screaming into his phone, sweating bullets, Dorothy crying in the corner.

Joe messaged:

[JOE] The seeds are in. The Yakuza want blood. Dorothy's parents hired a lawyer. Alec's assistant just sold a photo of him passed out drunk to TMZ. Enjoy the popcorn.

[ME] I'm on broccoli.

Outside, the world turned.

Kids screamed. The rice cooker and the oven beeped. The scent of garlic and Korean spicy ramen filled the air. And in the shadows of a suburban kitchen…

An empire fell. Piece by piece. To the woman no one saw coming.

*****

Jaya's birthday was coming.

And I was not okay. I stood in the middle of my very clean, very beige living room, holding a pink unicorn paper plate with shaking hands and muttering like I'd just been asked to plan the Olympics.

"A party?" I mumbled to myself. "With… balloons? Kids? Games?"

I was sweating like a fugitive in a TSA line.

I had faced global smugglers, buried weapons in dead zones, laundered millions across continents with nothing but a flip phone and a lipstick knife — but this?

This was parental hell.

"JHING!" I screamed into my phone like it was on fire. "I NEED HELP."

She and Mylene arrived at my house in matching green Crocs and clipboards. They looked too serious, like it was about dead dinosaurs or something related to world peace.

"I got this," Jhing Jhing said with military-grade confidence.

"First, colour theme. Unicorns or dinosaurs?" Mylene asked, sipping a juice pouch she stole from my fridge.

"Can't we just give the kids snacks and throw them in the backyard?"

They both stared at me like I had suggested sacrificing a puppy.

"NO." Next thing I knew, my house was covered in catalogues.
Balloon swatches.
Disney Theme sample books.
And Disney Cake testers.

"Cake comes in four tiers now?" I gasped. "It's for a toddler! She eats crayons!"

Jhing Jhing didn't blink. "Are you crazy? She's your girl now. And your girl deserves a Disney cake the size of a smart car."

"But…"

"No buts. Sure, you can afford it, right?" Mylene asked.

"Yes."

"Then it's a four layered Peppa Pig cake."

Meanwhile, Jhing had created a guest list spreadsheet. There were tabs. Colour codes. Backup RSVPs. I hadn't used Excel since my alias hacked a Belgian bank. I told the moms that my second lottery win helped fund the event.

"It wasn't a lot. You know. Just enough for a small party. And a backup generator. And a face-painting clown imported from France."

THE DAY OF THE PARTY

It was mayhem. Pink Pig, Unicorns and dinosaurs had fused into one chaotic hybrid theme:

"PIGUNICOSAUR MAYHEM" — a glitter-drenched apocalypse of cuteness.

God. My head ached so much I could have used vodka but here I was, holding a pink little piggy cup with green blue liquid that tastes like wet cotton candy-sugar and diabetes.

The backyard had become a war zone of bouncy castles, bubble machines, and inflatable axolotls (I still don't know why those were there).

Mylene manned the face-painting table with a trembling brush. Jhing Jhing was shouting in three languages, trying to herd kids away from the chocolate fountain and peanut butter sandwich. I was dressed in a pastel blue and pink hoodie that said "PIGGY PARTY SQUAD" — I hated it.

My kitchen counters were buried under pink 60 juice boxes, 100 blue and green cupcakes, two coolers full of pink soda, and three platters of organic, gluten-free, soy-hugged, nut-free snacks that no child wanted. Cookies, nuts, chips, fries and I swear I saw candies the size of my head.

But the kids were having the time of their lives. Jaya was screaming with joy, covered in rainbow cake, one shoe missing, riding a balloon pink piggy like a horse.

Aliya was trying to convince other girls to start a cult made of glitter glue and lollipops.

Maya had a face painted like a lion, roaring at every adult who came too close.

For once, the chaos was worth it.

Until he showed up.

It was close to sunset. The kids were winding down. The clown had just finished his final magic trick — pulling a rubber chicken from someone's pants — when the front gate slammed open.

A tall man, shirt wrinkled, hair greasy, eyes glassy and wild, stormed in like he owned the place.

"JAAAAAAKE!" he bellowed.

A little boy holding a rainbow cupcake dropped it.

"Daddy?"

"I told you not to come!" the boy's mother whispered, standing behind me, pale.

He marched across the yard, stinking of cheap whiskey and anger.

"You think I'm going to let you steal my son?" he screamed, shoving through the crowd. "You rich pricks think I don't matter?"

Parents froze. Kids whimpered.

And then—he slapped Mylene hard when she raised her brow at him.

Her face whipped sideways. She stumbled, holding her cheek in stunned silence. The bounce house deflated like a dying animal. Jaya screamed.

I blacked out for half a second. Because when I came to — I was already moving.

Like death wearing mom-pink jeans.

"Hey!" I roared.

He turned toward me, just as my fist collided with his jaw. A clean, sharp snap echoed through the backyard.

The crowd gasped.

"WHAT THE—?"

"You don't touch my friend," I growled, grabbing a bubble wand and smashing it across his shoulder. He tried to swing at me, but I ducked low — instinct and training kicking in.

My knee met his stomach. He doubled over.

I grabbed a decorative balloon stand, spun, and smashed it across his back like I was in an underground gladiator match.

Kids were crying. One kid was cheering. I think it was mine. He lunged again, swearing and bleeding from the lip.

But I sidestepped and—

POW! —landed a roundhouse kick.

His body flew sideways, landing in the unicorn cake. He didn't get back up. The music stopped. Silence fell. Then someone clapped.

The police came ten minutes later. Mylene was taken to urgent care — her cheek swollen, but she was okay.

The man? Hospitalized. Concussion. Broken ribs. Bruised ego.

I was handcuffed. "Yes, officer," I said calmly as they led me to the front yard. "I assaulted a man with a bubble wand and balloon stick. He hit my friend. And scared the children. I have no regrets."

One officer whispered to the other, "She's a badass."

They uncuffed me. Took my statement. Didn't arrest me. Mylene returned that night, wrapped in ice packs and fire in her eyes.

"Remind me to never cross you," she muttered, eating leftover pink cupcakes.

Jhing Jhing passed me a wine cooler and saluted. "You are now the Queen of Pig-Unicorn Brawls."

Later that night, when the kids were asleep and the yard looked like a warzone of party cups and shredded glitter banners, I sat on the porch.

I opened my secret laptop.

The screen showed Alec's mansion — panic, arguments, lawyers storming in and out.

I smirked.

Then I looked at the bruises on my knuckles and the weight loss app that congratulated me on 27 pounds gone.

I was changing. Faster than anyone expected. But not softer. Never that. Just sharper. Cleaner. And ready. Because this birthday may have ended in chaos—

But the real party was just beginning.

It was just after midnight. The apartment was quiet. The kind of eerie, tense quiet that seeps through walls like a ghost holding its breath.

The kids were asleep — sprawled on their beds like little warriors resting after a chaotic party war. Jaya still had pink frosting in her hair. Maya was wrapped like a burrito in three blankets. Aliya had insisted on sleeping with a plastic sword tucked beside her pillow "in case the cake man comes back."

I was in the garage, sipping black coffee in my secure, military-grade underground office — the hum of screens lighting my face. Alec's security feeds danced in front of me like a digital opera. His house was chaos. Traitors, broken shipments, and a PR disaster eating him alive. I had just started decrypting a Yakuza meeting ledger when my phone buzzed.

Ray.

I blinked. What the hell was he doing at this hour? And why was he calling at 12:17 a.m.?

I let it ring. Then it rang again. Twelve times.

Damn it! With a sigh deep enough to shake tectonic plates, I answered. "What?"

Ray's voice came out panicked. Desperate. "I—I need help."

I froze.

He was supposed to be in Alaska. Whale-watching. Shark-fishing. Cousin-hugging. Whatever ridiculous lie he'd cooked up this time. "What happened?" I asked flatly.

"I'm in trouble," he whispered. "I… I owe money."

I stood, slowly. My back cracked. My pulse slowed. "How much money, Ray?"

Silence. Then— "One hundred and eighty thousand pounds."

I let out a single, low laugh. "That's not debt, Ray. That's a death sentence."

He came home the next day. Looking like hell's least successful janitor. Hair greasy. Shirt wrinkled. A casino wristband still clinging to his arm like a scarlet letter.

"I swear, I was going to win it back," he mumbled. "I just— I didn't know the casino changed ownership."

My eyes narrowed. The bastard. How could he be this stupid.

"What casino?"

He looked up sheepishly. "The... the one um, that dead billionaire used to manage under that alias—uh—Bella Thorne?"

What the hell? I nearly choked. "That was never his alias, Ray. That's a Disney star."

"Oh, but how did you know that?" he muttered.

"It doesn't matter, Jesus. How could you lose so much?" I gripped the back of the kitchen chair. "You gambled away nearly one hundred thousand at Alec Darrow's casino?" The one he stole from me? The one that I left rigged with a silent alert system the second someone used a last-name-only ID to open a VIP tab?

Ray's face lost colour.

I gave him a withering look. I sat him down. For a minute he was like a lost wet chicken. I gave him fruit juice. He was shaking like a cold ferret in a paper bag.

"Ray," I said gently. "How long have you been gambling?"

He couldn't meet my eyes. "Since before Maya was born."

"How much have you lost?"

"...Over half a million."

My teeth clenched. My fists curled. I wasn't even angry — not in the explosive way I'd been when Alec kissed Dorothy, or when that drunk dad ruined the birthday.

This was different. This was a quiet kind of rage. This body remembered the pain, the betrayal.

Chapter 11

The next morning started with cereal spilled on the floor, Maya screaming about her missing hairbrush, and Jaya trying to flush a plastic pony down the toilet.

I was halfway through brushing my teeth when I heard the unmistakable crash of porcelain in the kitchen. "Aliya! What did I say about climbing the shelves?!"

She peeked around the corner, her curls full of flour. "I was trying to make pancakes for you, Mommy."

"…With the cat?"

"No! The cat was just helping!"

The cat—bless his confused soul—was covered in powdered sugar and looked like a very sad ghost.

Then I saw Ray. Slouched on the couch. In his boxer shorts. Scratching his stomach.

Like a leftover mistake I kept forgetting to throw out. And suddenly, the mental image of him gambling away half a million pounds in my old casino burned through me like battery acid.

I wasn't sure if I wanted to smother him with a pillow or stuff a broccoli down his throat.

Ray.
The man who'd gone through my drawers looking for spare change. Who left his crusty socks on the dining

table. Who had the audacity to lose half a million in the casino I used to own before Alec took it.

And now he had the nerve to breathe loudly near my coffee.

"I swear, I'm done with casinos," he said, not even looking up from his phone. "I got a trucking gig starting tomorrow. Long haul. I'll be gone two weeks."

My eyebrow twitched.

"Gone-gone?"

"Yup. Alaska first. Then cross-border stuff. I even bought a new map."

You'd think he'd told me he was going to save a dying orphan, the way he looked so proud of himself. I sipped my black coffee, hot and bitter, just like me. "As long as you're not going to the casino again."

"No. No more gambling. I'm a changed man."

"You said that last time. You even got a tattoo of a dice and 'NO REGERTS'."

Ray paused, then nodded solemnly. "That's true. That was before I hit rock bottom."

I took another sip. This time, I imagined it was wine. A whole bottle.

*****

Mylene dropped by with fresh bread and a bag full of donated baby clothes. Bless her soul. We were sorting socks by size when Maya ran past screaming, "JAYA PUT GLITTER IN MY UNDERWEAR!"

Ray was in the background watching Die Hard and chewing cereal straight from the box.

Mylene leaned close and whispered, "Girl, how have you not poisoned him yet?"

"I almost did last week. But the bleach bottle had a baby safety lock."

"I can help with that," she offered, half-serious.

We both laughed too hard.

Meanwhile, Jhing Jhing called, frantically reminding me about the school PTA costume drive. Apparently, I volunteered.

Me. The bringer of chaos and guns. Volunteered.

When the kids were finally passed out—Jaya on the floor hugging a wet shoe, Aliya halfway off the couch, and Maya snoring under a blanket fort—I tucked them in and escaped to my room.

Ray was asleep. Snoring like a dying moose.

I carefully tiptoed around his mountain of dirty laundry and locked myself in the bathroom with my laptop.

The screen lit up. I opened my encrypted vault. A list of offshore transfers flickered back at me.

Everything was working.

The properties were sold. Now, the Chinese and Korean were suspicious of Alec. The media was circling like sharks.

And now, I had to decide which thread to pull next. I decided to go take the money back Ray easily lost. I will go there myself and gamble my way in. But before I could plan, a notification blinked on my phone. Ray had texted me—from across the apartment.

[Ray]: hey u seen my trucker boots?

I stared at the screen. He was ten feet away. I could hear him breathing.

And that was the moment I knew… He needed to leave. Not tomorrow. Now.

The next morning, I helped him pack.

"Well, don't you seem eager," he said, shoving his duffel into the hallway.

"I'm just excited for your fresh start, Ray."

He blinked. "You called me Ray."

I smiled. "Slip of the tongue."

He kissed my cheek.

I stiffened like a corpse. What the fuck? I really wanted to kill this man. How dare he!

He chuckled. "Still don't like it when I do that, huh?"

"Not unless you want to lose teeth."

He laughed, thinking I was joking.

I wasn't. Hell, right there, I want to just slit his throat.

Finally, he got into his old truck and drove away, off to chase something that wasn't me, and for once—I breathed.

The apartment felt ten sizes larger without his stale presence. The kids were still chaotic, of course. But now, I had space.

To plan. To move. To burn Alec's world from the ground up. And this time… no snoring truck driver would get in my way.

It all started at 7:46 AM on a Wednesday.

The coffee hadn't even kicked in. My youngest was doing battle with a pancake that was somehow both burned and raw, while Maya screamed about a missing sock that was right on her foot.

Jhing Jhing sat on my couch like a zombie in pyjamas, holding a baby bottle she mistook for her coffee mug. Mylene was already two steps away from crying because her toddler glued cereal to the TV again.

Then I said the words that would change the course of history.

"I need a makeover."

Silence.

Utter. Pure. Stone-cold silence. Even the cat stopped chewing on the curtains.

Jhing Jhing's eyes twitched. "A what?"

"I need to look like a goddess."

Mylene blinked rapidly. "Did you hit your head? Are you okay? Blink twice if this is a cry for help."

I slammed my spoon down. I've already told them about Ray's losing money in the casino. "I'm going to the casino, and I plan to win big. But to do that, I need to walk in like a storm in a dress. Like thunder with lipstick. Like vengeance wrapped in silk."

More silence.

Then Mylene snorted so hard she nearly fell off the couch. "You? In a dress?"

Jhing Jhing laughed so hard she choked on her cereal. "You haven't worn a dress since Maya was born. You wear sneakers to funerals."

"Exactly. No one will see it coming."

I raised a single perfectly unplucked eyebrow. "You two will come with me. We will win."

"How? I'm not good at math." Mylene asked, eyeing the biscuit stuck in the baby chair.

Jhing Jhing added, "I'm not lucky as well."

"Don't worry. I can win. I promise, plus, I'm paying. Salon. Spa. Shoes. Shimmer. Everything."

They both sat up straight like I'd said, "Free cake."

That was easy.

We stormed into the boutique like a tornado wearing sunglasses.

The saleswoman—immaculately polished and clearly allergic to children—took one look at the juice-box-covered kids trailing us and said, "Can I help you?"

"Yes," I replied, "I want a dress that screams: I'm rich, beautiful, and might stab someone."

She blinked. "So... bold?"

"Deadly."

Few minutes later, the kids were thrown into the nursing room with cookies and soda and with their part-time nannies.

Mylene ran to a rack of sequined gowns and began twirling them like a Disney villain. "Ooooh, what about THIS? You'll blind a man from thirty feet!"

"No sequins. I'm not a disco ball. I need something classy."

Jhing Jhing appeared holding a red dress with a neckline so low it needed a warning label. "What about this one? This will make the patron's jaw drop."

"That's not a dress. That's dental floss with ambition."

We fought. Oh, how we fought.

There were ten rejected dresses. One got stuck over my head and I swore I almost died. Another was so tight I couldn't breathe and Jhing Jhing had to unzip me while Mylene held my arms back like we were exorcising a demon.

Finally, I found it. And they found something for themselves as well.

After two hours.

What I got was a sleek, backless black number with a slit high enough to make angels weep. It fit like it had been made for me—hugging all the right curves, making me look like money and revenge had a baby.

"Oh damn," Mylene whispered. "This is a dress that starts wars."

"I look like a Bond villain," I said.

"Correction: a Bond villain with custody of the kids."

Then a few minutes later, after yet another scream from Jaya and a milk bottle mishap from Ivy, we stumbled into the designer shoe store next. That's where things went off the rails.

And then—*heels shopping.*

Heels. Heels everywhere.

Can I even handle that weapon? Me the badass of all badasses in heels?

Of course.

Maybe not.

Glitter. Gold. Studded. Laced. Stilettos that looked like medieval weapons.

Mylene tried on a pair of six-inch boots and immediately fell on her butt. "Okay. These are trying to murder me."

Jhing Jhing held up thigh-high boots and grinned. "I can't feel my toes but I look like Beyoncé."

I found a pair of black stilettos with silver trim—sharp enough to count as a concealed weapon.

"These," I said.

The saleslady nodded solemnly. "Those are called the Widowmaker 3000."

"Perfect."

No. It was very far from perfect.

The horror.

How do women walk in these things? They're not shoes, they're medieval stilts for fashion gladiators. I put on one glittery death trap and nearly dislocated my spine. "You'll get used to it!" Mylene said while balancing like a gymnast. I looked like a baby giraffe trying to stand on an ice rink.

By the time we reached the dress section, I was emotionally broken. Sequins. Slits. Cleavage. I'd worn combat armour more comfortable than this. But the worst part?

I saw myself in the mirror.

And... I didn't look like a monkey out of the forest anymore. I didn't look like Catherine-the-barely-functioning-mom, or the woman who once googled "what is a lip stain and is it fatal?"

No. I looked hot.

Like walk-into-a-casino-and-make-men-weep hot.

"Damn," Jhing Jhing said.

"You dress up too well," Mylene added.

Then I almost tripped on my heels and broke a mannequin.

But if the boutique was madness, the salon was war.

We booked a "VIP Triple Treatment" at a high-end place downtown.

They were not ready. The moment they saw us and the kids (whom I had bribed with emergency iPads and gummy bears), the staff collectively sighed like soldiers marching into battle.

Then waxing.

"Let's start with her," one stylist said, pointing at me.

"No waxing," I growled. "You try waxing my eyebrows and I will file a complaint to the United Nations."

"Understood. Just threading."

Of course they didn't listen.

Few seconds later. I swear I saw angels. How could someone get through that torture? And they call this pampering?

Hell. If this wasn't torture, I don't know what is anymore. Forget waterboarding, forget military interrogation—try getting your leg hair ripped out by a woman named Daisy who smiles like she's snacking on your screams.

"I promise it's not that bad!" Mylene had said, like a traitor. "It's just a wax."

WAX, she said.

They should call it Skin-Ripping Hell Melted From Satan's Armpit. I was gripping the edge of the spa bed like I was about to give birth to a cactus.

"Breathe," Daisy cooed, applying the next patch.

I did breathe. I breathed fire. I swore. I screamed. I saw the face of every enemy I've ever made—and whispered promises of vengeance with each yank.

Meanwhile, Jhing Jhing was beside me, in a fluffy white robe, sipping lemon cucumber detox water like she was royalty reborn. "This is self-care," she said. SELF-CARE.

Self-care, my ass.

Then came the *facial*.

I thought that meant cucumber slices and relaxing music. No. That was a *lie* sold by movies. This one involved a machine that hissed steam into my face like a dragon burping rage. Then some sort of tool that felt like a miniature chainsaw scraped at my pores while a woman named Giselle whispered about exfoliating layers of sin from my past lives.

"Oh, your skin's dry," she said.

Of course it's dry! I've aged ten years in thirty minutes!

Then the hair.

It wasn't that bad.

"I want curls," I said with the confidence of a warrior.

"Soft and bouncy?"

"No. Dangerously seductive. Like I sell poison for fun."

"Copy that, sister."

When I looked around, I saw an imposing, blond woman entered the office. In contrast to the girl by the window's flamboyance, she dressed solemnly in black, which contrasted sharply with her pale skin.

"I'm Santy, dear," she said as she entered the room. "I do hair and makeup." She placed a huge make-up case on the carpet, then opened it to retrieve a hair brush and drier. "Please have a seat, sweetie."

I nodded and bit my lips. Of course, they have their own fashionistas—very cool make-up artists that even Paris Hilton would envy. I sat in one of the office chairs, meticulously altering my clothes so I didn't show too much skin.

I, the assassin, the kingpin, Leon Darrow, finally succumbed to hair and makeup. My hair was fluffed around my shoulders by the girl. And I swear it felt like forever.

"It shouldn't be too fine or too thick. Your hair is amazing. Is this your natural skin tone?"

"Yes," I replied. Thanks to Catherine's hidden gem.

"Lovely, you have very healthy hair, dear," she said as she combed the brush over my hair, teasing out some snarls.

"Thank you."

Then the makeup.

"Just a little makeup, okay?" I spoke.

Santy blinked. "Of course, sweetheart. *Just a little*," she murmured in response as she looked through her make-up case. Brandishing a pair of tweezers, she said, "You know what, girl? Your skin is like fine porcelain; to cover it with anything would be a sin. Such amazing skin. I love it." With a deft touch, she plucked my eyebrows. I screamed. Then I sat like a hostage while another woman approached with a collection of brushes and creams like she was going to paint the Mona Lisa on my forehead.

"What's your usual makeup routine?" she asked.

"I Google 'how not to look dead' and hope for the best," I replied.

"Oh, honey," she said, and that was it. That was the moment I lost my dignity.

She went in like Michelangelo at war. Which, in beauty-speak, apparently meant: foundation, concealer, primer, bronzer, highlighter, three types of blushes, two types of mascara, something called 'baking powder' that's not even edible, and a setting spray that made me feel like I was being lacquered for display. Lashes longer than my fingers. I couldn't blink without feeling like a ceiling fan. I sneezed and the highlighter on my cheek reflected light into another dimension.

"Please take it easy on me," I begged and sneezed again, and the glitter on my cheeks caught the light like a disco ball at a rave.

"Absolutely, girl,"

To say I was happy and disappointed at the same time was an understatement. Yes, they pampered me, but Jesus, the pain was too much! To ignore the pain, I asked, "Santy, have you worked here for a long time?" I winced. What I really wanted to learn and know was how someone ended up torturing their client but I wasn't willing to say it so directly.

"Years and years, dear! This is like my life," she said, returning the tweezers to her case and selecting an eye makeup palette. She applied eyeshadow quickly, followed by liner and mascara.

You might wonder how I've known those silly things?

Ha! I've googled everything yesterday—from "how to contour a double chin" to "difference between eyebrow pencil and eyeliner". I couldn't risk my identity as Catherine if I looked like Tarzan or a monkey fresh out of the forest, blinking at civilization, who doesn't know those very important silly things they called make-up and pencil.

I even watched a twelve-year-old beauty guru on YouTube do a full glam look in eight minutes. I've never thought that in my entire life I'd be googling things like "what is a setting spray" or "can mascara kill you if you stab your eye?"

The last touch was a little coat of lipstick. I glimpsed glances of myself in the little mirror connected to her make-up bag as she worked. The lipstick hue complimented my natural lip tone, adding a little pop of colour. Woah! I am beautiful! I mean, of course I am beautiful; my kids, I mean, Catherine's kids used to say that all the time, but now... This is a different kind of beauty, and I'm happy about it. This body was happy.

I nodded to myself.

"You're all set, darling," she mumbled, cleaning up her supplies

The woman who looked back at me was tall and pretty. My eyelashes were almost as long as Jhing Jhing now, and there was a pink glow to my skin. You would never know I had fat pants at home. Or that my idea of dressing up was wearing faded mama jeans, a T-shirt, and an old Nike from Catherine's closet.

Somehow, I'd been transformed into the supermodel fantasy version of Catherine.

Woah! This was next-level shit!

Am I scared? Yes.

Am I foolish to go through all that torture? Yes.

I thought it would require plastic surgery, but all I needed was the appropriate hair and make-up. Huh. So, there you have it.

Chapter 12

Meanwhile…Jhing Jhing was yelling at a colourist. "You turned me ORANGE!"

Mylene was arguing about lipstick. "I said Blood Red, not 'Berry Bliss'! I'm not here to look edible, I'm here to look expensive!"

It was a three-hour storm of hairspray, bobby pins, nail polish, and death threats.

Jhing Jhing peeked over from the next chair and burst out laughing. "You look like a Bond villain's ex-wife who came back for revenge."

"Exactly the look I was going for," I muttered, trying not to lick the lip gloss that felt like someone had glued strawberry jelly to my face.

Mylene, who'd already gone through her transformation and looked like she walked off the cover of Vogue for Agents, gave me a thumbs up. "You're killing it."

I stared into the mirror again.

My hair flowed in shimmering waves, like I had my own wind machine following me around. My lashes were so long I was sure they could cause a windstorm if I blinked fast enough. My cheekbones were sculpted by the hands of makeup demigods, and my lips? Red. Glossy. Dangerous. Like I'd kissed a Ferrari.

"I look… expensive," I whispered.

"You look terrifyingly beautiful," Santy corrected, proud like a mother hen. "Now go put on that beautiful dress, the one with the slit up to your liver."

Oh, right. The dress.

Jhing Jhing brought it out, holding it with the reverence of someone carrying a holy relic. "Are you sure about this? It's basically two napkins held together by prayer and spaghetti straps."

"Perfect," I said grimly. "If I'm going to rob a casino blind, I might as well blind them with my thighs."

So, we squeezed into our outfits. Correction: we fought our way into them. Jhing Jhing was doing lunges just to zip hers up.

Mylene tried jumping while screaming, "Why do I feel like a sausage in a casing?!"

I was sweating like a convict at a lie detector test by the time mine was on, but once I stood up?

Oh, yeah. We didn't look like three tired moms on a mission. We looked like we were about to bankrupt a nation.

Jhing Jhing's new honey-blonde waves glowed under the salon lights.

Mylene's smoky eyes could kill a man in an alley.

And me? I was a dark flame in a velvet storm.

When it was all done, we looked like gods. And I swear, something in me was happy, this body remembered something from maybe, old days, it was happy. I am happy. I looked good. Catherine looked good.

We strutted out of the salon like a pack of lions on a catwalk. People stared.

One guy dropped his coffee.

A kid on a scooter literally ran into a bench. The guy at the exit did a double take so hard, his hat fell off.

It was glorious. Let them sweat. Because the three extra-large magnets had arrived. And we were ready to attract chaos.

And that evening, with three babysitters in my apartment, our kids were loaded with donuts, pizza, ice cream and more candies. We walked out in slow motion, like the trailer to a summer blockbuster no one saw coming.

People stopped and stared. A valet walked into a lamppost.

Even the car alarms went off. I opened the door of the SUV like a queen entering a battlefield.

"Let's go win some money," I said.

Mylene slid in beside me. "You look like you belong in a spy movie."

Jhing Jhing grinned. "No. She looks like the final boss."

I smirked.

"Good."

The Grand Entrance.

We didn't walk into the high-roller floor. We descended like gods with credit limits.

The moment the elevator doors opened, the symphony of money greeted us—slot machines ringing like bells in a cathedral, cards shuffling like whispers of fate, the low murmur of wealth, and the occasional laugh of someone who hadn't yet realized they were losing their mortgage.

All eyes turned.

Mylene, dressed in shimmering silver, winked at a pit boss like she owned him. Earlier she said about how sexy she was and something like "I'm not plus-size, I'm just easy to see from afar." And yes, I agree, she was hot. In a way she had curves in all the right places.

Jhing Jhing, in fire-red silk and heels that could impale a man, strutted like it was Paris Fashion Week. And while we were all busy earlier? She said that she was not fat at all. God loves her so much that He decided to supersize her. That's my girl. Her confidence was top notch.

And me? I was death in black velvet, with a slit up to heaven and lips painted in blood promises.

Though I'm still in a large size era, take note, not extra-large anymore, curves are my fashion superpower, and I'm not afraid to flaunt them. I am Leon Darrow for a reason.

I raised my brows as I looked around those vultures.

Those whispers rose like smoke. Who were we? Why were we here?

Then I caught his eyes. One of Alec's men. Mick. My former surveillance operator, now wearing a cheap suit two sizes too small and a name tag that said "Casino Loyalty Officer."

Poor guy. He narrowed his eyes as if he'd seen a ghost—but I tilted my chin, laughed lightly, and said to a nearby wealthy patron in a fake posh voice, "Well, when you win the lottery, darling, you have to celebrate."

The rich man nodded appreciatively.

Mick? He smirked. That knowing smirk. The kind that said: "Ah, tourists."

I could see it all in his smug little face: three overdressed women who didn't know blackjack from baklava.

Three walking, talking bank accounts for the casino to bleed dry. And that's when I knew I had him. We walked right past him.

Mylene nudged me. "Did he buy it?"

I grinned. "Oh, he bought it and gift-wrapped it for Christmas."

Jhing Jhing snorted. "Great. Now tell me again— how exactly are we not losing everything we own tonight?"

I touched the gold bracelet on my wrist—the same bracelet Alec once gave me when I "accidentally" saved his life during a yacht shootout off the coast of Marseille. Funny how things circle back.

"Trust me," I told the girls, my voice low and confident. "Just go with the flow. Follow my lead."

They nodded, heels clicking with mine in perfect sync as we made our entrance to the high-roller floor.

And let me be clear—we didn't walk in. We arrived.

It was like the casino itself paused to catch its breath.

Three women dressed in danger and dripping in designer. Hair perfectly tousled, makeup sharp enough to commit federal crimes. Our dresses shimmered with every step—liquid silk in deep crimson, emerald green, and midnight black. Each slit, strap, and open back strategically chosen to make powerful men forget how to count.

Jhing Jhing's dress clung to her like a second skin and sculpted to her every generous curve. She looked like a goddess who'd come down from Olympus just to empty your bank account. Her smile? Lethal. Her laugh? A siren's song that made two men crash into each other near the poker pit.

Mylene's smile highlighted her dusky skin like moonlight on obsidian. Her neckline dipped low enough to give a man religion. She played with the strap of her clutch absentmindedly, the way one might fiddle with a dagger.

Me? I said I wasn't here to play—I was here to take souls and leave smudges of lipstick as my signature. We moved like synchronized predators. Every head turned.

Men whispered. Women glared or stared—either in admiration or envy. We weren't just players.

We were the show.

First stop: Blackjack.

The table was dimly lit, like something out of a noir film. Velvet green felt. Polished mahogany trim. A gold plaque reading Minimum Bet: £5,000.

Perfect.

The dealer was new. You could smell the inexperience beneath the gallons of cheap cologne. He was young—maybe early twenties. Blond. Twitchy. Sweated like he'd just been caught texting the boss's wife.

He gave us a stiff nod. "Ladies."

I smiled, trailing my fingers across the table like a caress. "Gentlemen," I purred to no one in particular.

Around us, the sharks circled. Two older men in tailored suits. One with a pinky ring so large it could knock someone out. The other with the dead eyes of someone who used to run black market deals in Prague.

I sat, slowly, crossing my legs so the slit in my dress did all the talking. "Let's play." I placed a moderate bet. Just enough to look confident. Not too much to draw suspicion.

He dealt.

Queen of Hearts.

I looked at him. Straight in the eyes. Winked.

Poor guy.

He twitched. Then he gave me a five.

I bit my bottom lip and sipped my wine. "Oh my," I said sweetly. "How lucky."

Dealer coughed. Pinky Ring cleared his throat. Someone behind us muttered a soft curse.

Mylene was next. She leaned forward just enough for the lights to catch the glitter in her cleavage. "Hit me," she said, voice sultry as silk.

She had a twelve.

He hesitated.

She giggled, and then blew a kiss to the man seated beside us. "Don't worry, I'm lucky tonight."

He gave her a nine.

She flashed a dazzling smile. "Told you."

Now Jhing—Jhing didn't flirt. She challenged. She glared at the cards like they owed her money.

Two eights. She slammed her chips down. "Split."

Both hands?

Face cards.

Dealer bust.

We didn't squeal. We didn't cheer. We smiled like women who had been here before. Like winning was expected.

We stood up, hips swaying like a pendulum of doom, and left the table £15,000 richer after just three hands.

The crowd parted for us like we were royalty walking through peasants.

At the bar, Mick was watching. I felt his gaze before I saw him. His eyes narrowed. He knew us. Or thought he did. He once guarded the private vault. Now he was Alec's eyes on the floor.

He tilted his head and smirked. Probably thought we were just three flashy women who got lucky. Lottery winners. Rich bored housewives. A walking cliché.

Good. Let him think that. Let him underestimate us.

Mylene raised her glass toward him with a wink. Jhing adjusted her earring with a sigh like she was already tired of winning. I flicked my hair over my shoulder and made sure the gold bracelet caught the light.

I built this floor. I programmed the system. I coded the dealers tells and rigged the RFID chips in the roulette tables years ago. This was my house. And tonight?

Tonight, I came back to collect.

Next stop: Roulette. Now this was where the magic happened. The roulette system had a slight delay between spin registration and number declaration on the floor display. Most wouldn't notice. But I had a signal sent through my discreetly modified smartwatch, connected to a lag exploit I programmed years ago.

It wasn't cheating, per se. It was… remembering the flaws I left behind.

Forgotten cracks in the system, whispers in code, and lazy updates by people too afraid or too dumb to erase my signature. I placed a fat stack of chips on "Red 19."

Jhing Jhing laughed like she picked the number on a whim, twirling a loose curl of her hair as if she was deciding between tea flavours. "Ohh, Red 19 just feels... spicy."

The croupier gave her a polite, confused smile. He was young—maybe early twenties—with slicked-back hair and a jawline that looked chiselled by debt. His white gloves trembled for a split second as he picked up the ivory ball. I caught it.

He knew. Not what, but something.

Maybe it was our confidence.

Maybe the way I watched the wheel—not like a gambler, but like an engineer.

He spun the wheel. The lights above reflected in the polished mahogany. The ball clattered, skipped, danced its chaotic ballet.

And then it landed.

Red 19.

"Winner," the croupier said, trying to keep his voice level, but I caught the shift—his eyes widened a fraction too long before the training kicked in. He cleared his throat. "Payout, 35 to 1."

Chips slid across the felt toward us like obedient soldiers. The sound was a lullaby of vengeance.

Across the room, I felt it. The mood.

The men. Their gazes lingered—not the usual lecherous weight women endure in heels and lipstick.

No, this was something more... primal.

Confusion. Jealousy. Hunger. We weren't three bimbos blowing lottery cash anymore.

We were sharks in sequins. I saw one older man—Rolex, wine gut, too much cologne—lean over to his friend and whisper, "They're on fire." The friend shook his head slowly, like he was watching a miracle unfold. Or a train wreck he couldn't look away from.

Mylene smiled sweetly and bent over the table, enough to make even the statues blush. "Let's do another," she purred, pretending to bite her nail. "How about... Black 17?"

The dealer looked paler than before. That twitch in his left cheek returned. He was sweating. His gloved hand trembled just slightly, but enough for me to clock it.

He spun again. The room around us held its breath. Cards shuffled from distant tables. Cocktail waitresses floated past with trays of overpriced fantasy. Somewhere, a jackpot bell rang, but it sounded like a child's toy in comparison to this moment.

The ball danced.

Slowed.

Black 17.

Mylene squealed, doing a little shimmy of fake surprise. "Oh my god, did I really just—"

The croupier cleared his throat. "Winner."

Jhing Jhing slapped the table. "Buy me a yacht!"

Laughter erupted. From us, and—begrudgingly—from the men watching. A few clapped. Some were leaning forward now. Others weren't smiling anymore. Their chips sat untouched as they stared.

They weren't sure whether to flirt or fear us. I could taste the tension. It rolled off the walls like heat from a kitchen. By now, even I was feeling giddy.

Not from the money. Please. It was the power. The reclamation. It was mine, this casino. Once upon a time. And now, here I was—winning my way through the gilded halls of my past with two glamazon best friends and a dress that made men walk into chairs.

"Another drink?" a waiter asked, tall and awkward, holding a tray with crystal glasses and too much cologne.

I turned, flashed a grin, and purred, "No, darling. I need all my brain cells for math."

Mylene giggled like a schoolgirl. Jhing Jhing raised her glass, sipping mocktail like it was poison. "She's dangerous when she starts calculating."

The croupier finally spoke, soft and clipped, "Ladies... would you like to continue?"

"Oh, sweetheart," I said, stacking chips like a warlord lining up artillery, "we haven't even started."

Craps was always the loudest table, the wildest game. Perfect cover.

I nudged Jhing Jhing to roll.

"You want me to throw dice?"

"Yup."

"I haven't rolled dice since Monopoly in 2003!"

"Just act drunk and follow my finger."

Thanks to an old mechanic that still existed—table tilt awareness—I could signal which side the die was more likely to land using pressure memory on the felt and the angle of the corner bumpers.

She rolled.

"Seven!"

Cheers.

Then again.

"Eleven!"

A man next to us muttered, "These women are on fire."

"You have no idea," I murmured. The neckline plunged almost to my belly button, and the key to keeping my breasts covered was tying the halter tight behind my neck. The slit stopped about six inches before my pubic mound. I would have to be careful when I walked, or my vagina would play peek-a-boo with everyone I met.

By the third hour, we had amassed nearly £275,000.

And now? Now Mick was frowning.

He started talking into his radio, eyeing every dealer we touched. Two security officers subtly circled our area. One even fake-stumbled just to check my bracelet.

Fools.

That bracelet was not tech—it just connected to the heel of my shoe, which housed the real transmitter. My feet hurt, yes, but it was worth it.

Mylene whispered, "They're onto us."

I nodded. "Let them watch."

Then I took out my phone—the old one. Burnt-looking. Clunky.

The one connected to my private server hidden in Greece.

And I tapped a button labelled:

"Gambit Protocol: Disperse Winnings. Dummy Win Registered. Lock Surveillance Loop."

The cameras would now play a 15-minute loop of our past behaviour while we moved to the VIP vault payout room.

I leaned into the table, gave Mick a wink, and said, "Well, it's been fun, but I think it's time for champagne and a cashout."

He sneered.

"Of course, ma'am. Right this way."

Chapter 13

In the payout vault, we were handed our cash. Bundles. Stacks. Thick envelopes filled with dirty, glorious casino money. They wanted us gone before they figured out what we'd done.

Mick smiled politely, but I saw the twitch in his jaw.

"Have a good night, ladies," he said.

"Oh," I said, "we will."

As the elevator doors closed, I looked into the mirrored panel and whispered to myself:

"This place used to be Alec's."

Pause.

"Now it's mine again."

We didn't speak much on the drive home. Not because we didn't have anything to say—but because the girls were in shock. I pretended to be in shock as well.

£275,000. Freaking. Pounds.

From three hands of blackjack. No guns. No bloodshed. No broken bones. Just cleavage, eyeliner, and sass.

By the time we reached our building, reality hit Mylene and Jhing Jhing like a slow-motion slap. They just stared at each other inside the parked car like they had survived an alien abduction. I smirked at them.

They were amazing. Such innocence.

Then Jhing Jhing blurted, "Did we just commit legal robbery?"

Mylene shrieked. "We did! Oh my God, we just—did that! £275,000. pounds!" She clutched her pearls—literally, her fake pearl necklace had twisted during our victory strut and now looked like a noose of disbelief.

I was still gripping the steering wheel like I'd just outrun a SWAT team. "I think I blacked out after my Queen of Hearts," I muttered. "Was that a fever dream? Did we just—win?"

They were indeed so sweet.

To say that £275,000 made them so happy.

For me, it was just a penny but to them, it was like that world rained gold.

Jhing Jhing slapped the dashboard. "What do rich people eat after a win like that?! Champagne and caviar?!"

"No," I said solemnly, turning the key in the ignition again.

We all looked at each other.

And said in unison:

"McDonald's."

Fifteen minutes later, we marched into our tiny, chaotic apartment carrying three giant bags of fries, six burgers, two apple pies, three sundaes, and the kind of victorious madness usually reserved for lottery winners or deranged game show contestants.

We slammed everything onto the living room table like we had just looted a golden temple. Makeup still on. Heels tossed near the doorway. Jhing Jhing was half-sitting on the armrest like a queen with a paper crown made of napkins.

Mylene ripped into her burger with the kind of growl only heard in National Geographic documentaries. "I haven't had carbs like this since 2006."

"I feel like we should pray," I said dramatically, opening my fries like sacred scrolls.

"To what?" Jhing asked, mouth full of McChicken.

I raised my drink cup like a chalice. "To Blackjack Jesus. And the sacred dealer who couldn't read faces."

"To cleavage and bad cologne!" Mylene cheered, nearly choking on a fry.

We clinked our sodas like champagne flutes and dissolved into full-blown hysterical laughter.

And the laughter didn't stop. It rolled out of us like champagne foam—loud, bubbly, uncontrolled. Mylene wheezed until she fell sideways off the couch, Jhing laughed so hard she cried off her eyeliner, and I laughed until my stomach hurt, sprawled on the floor in a designer dress, barefoot and greasy-fingered.

We looked like we'd just returned from robbing the Queen's vault, not a casino.

My makeup was melting, my hair was falling apart, and I was balancing a cheeseburger on one hand like it was fine crystal.

But for the first time in what felt like years—I felt alive. This body felt alive. Catherine felt like she did it. She was happy. I am happy.

There were no bullets flying. No one screaming in the background. No betrayal looming like a shadow.

Just three girls. Fries. And a ridiculous, once-in-a-lifetime win that felt like justice in paper wrappers and barbecue sauce.

Outside, the city was cold and dark. But inside, we were glowing.

And as Jhing Jhing bit into a sundae spoon and whispered, "Let's do this again tomorrow…"

I smiled.

Oh, we will.

But next time?

We aim for more.

And maybe—just maybe—add chicken nuggets to the order.

The next night, we went again and this time, we wore sexier clothes than last night.

The chips kept piling. Like a fortress. Like a throne. Like revenge in glittering plastic circles. And believe me when I say this, I have more respect for women now that

I experience how to wear five-inch heels, the agony of waxing, hair fixing, not to mention the Spanx. Yes, it was a gift from the gods.

I sat straighter in my velvet chair, every movement intentional. The gown Mylene picked for me clung like sin—deep emerald green, backless, with a slit high enough to show I meant business and legs. And I swear, it took me two hours of practice to even walk from the weapon they called high heels. Somehow, Catherine's body remembered grace, feminine, remembered how to act like a seductress, remembered how to even smile like she owned the world. Indeed, she was something else. I am something else.

Mylene sparkled in rose gold, Jhing Jhing in scandalous red that made one man walk into a server carrying two glasses of scotch.

Clink—crash.

"Sorry, sir," the server muttered, but the man didn't even hear him. His eyes were locked on us. On me.

We were the three extra-large magnets. Not for metal, but for attention, desire, and suspicion.

And I felt it—the ripple effect. The discomfort. The envy.

It was intoxicating. Across the floor, a woman with a fur stole the size of a taxidermy bear narrowed her eyes. Her date, a wiry man in a navy suit, leaned so far in to get a better look at us that his wine tipped and soaked the cuff of his sleeve.

He didn't care.

"Who are they?" I imagined them whispering. "Why haven't we seen them before? Lottery winners? Movie stars?"

Wrong. We were ghosts dressed in Prada. My ghosts.

Then, the most important tell yet.

Mick. He was standing by the bar.

I hadn't seen him earlier, but I felt him before I spotted him. Tall, stocky, suspiciously bald—not by genetics but by choice, like he wanted to look more "military." He was the type of man who wore sunglasses indoors even when the ceiling was pure art deco and the lighting softer than a lover's sigh.

Mick had once worked directly under me. Casino security chief. A smart man, by the average IQ of thugs. Loyal—until Alec got his claws in him.

He had his phone to his ear.

His face said, "What the actual hell is going on."

I could tell by the way his fingers flexed. His jaw clenched. His eyes squinted in disbelief, like he was looking at an apparition. Not one woman, but three—each one tearing apart the night again like a well-dressed typhoon.

He turned his back toward the gaming floor and spoke low into his phone.

To Alec.

I knew it.

I didn't need confirmation.

He was probably saying, "Boss… you're not going to believe this, but the three biggest distractions I've ever seen just walked in again and are bleeding the tables dry. One of them… is the brain."

Me? BRAIN? OF COURSE I AM THE BRAIN. I AM DEATH with big boobies.

I am the ghost. The problem.

Then I smiled wider, like a woman who had never committed any crime worse than smiling too much in public. I waved at him.

Mick flinched.

The poor bastard flinched and pretended he wasn't looking at me. He turned back around, but his cover was blown.

Mylene noticed. "Hey, Cath... that bald dude's having a panic attack."

"That's Mick," I replied without moving my lips. "He's calling the monster."

Jhing Jhing tilted her head. "You mean Alec Darrow?"

"Mhmm."

"Oh, goodie," she muttered sarcastically. "Drama."

The croupier looked nervous.

Again.

By now, we were winning too much. Far more than probability allowed. But not enough to outright accuse us. Not yet.

Because see, I wasn't dumb enough to bet big every time.

No. I danced.

Again. Red 19, then nothing. Split 17-20, then skip a round. Small bets, big wins. Delay. Misdirect. Then a sweet gentle smile. Sip. Joke.

And of course… flirt. Subtly.

At one point, the older gentleman who'd been watching us sent over champagne.

I didn't drink it. I smiled and toasted with water.

"Trying to court a queen, is he?" Jhing Jhing whispered.

I smiled. "Poor man doesn't know this queen came to raze the kingdom."

The whispers grew louder. More eyes turned. Security started to linger too close.

"Should we worry?" Mylene asked, feigning innocence as she leaned closer.

"No," I said coolly, touching her hand like a doting friend. "Let them watch. That's the point."

And they did. They watched us like we were a headline unfolding in real time. Every man in the room saw not just three beautiful women—but danger. They saw luck too perfect, laughter too free, movements too precise.

And still, none of them could stop us. They didn't dare. Not yet.

At the bar, Mick ended the call. His face was pale.

I knew what Alec said on the other end. I could almost hear it.

"Don't touch her. Watch her. Record everything. I'm coming."

Perfect. I turned back to the table and picked up a fresh stack of chips.

"Ladies," I said, fire in my throat, "Let's win another hundred grand."

Jhing Jhing squealed. Mylene flipped her hair.

And the house—the very one I built—trembled.

Few minutes after yet another red wine we laughed and pretended, we couldn't handle alcohol. Of course, the girls couldn't. But I could.

An hour later, the lights above the high-stakes poker table shimmered like stars in a galaxy built on vice and victory. The velvet-lined chairs groaned under pressure; the polished mahogany table practically pulsed with tension. This was no ordinary game. This was war disguised as glamour.

Mylene clutched her designer clutch like it was a rosary. Jhing Jhing, already sweating, whispered in Tagalog, "Ate, are you sure? One million pounds? That's not just winning the lottery, that's... that's resurrection-level gambling!"

"Trust me," I said, voice a cool caress. "This is my cathedral. And tonight, we're saying mass."

Across the table, he emerged.

Alec.

But he didn't move.

Not yet.

He just stood there, watching me with the kind of patience only a predator could possess. His clothes were immaculate—dark, tailored perfection, the kind of wealth that radiated power in subtle, undeniable waves.

And the bastard was grinning like he already owned me.

The man who once begged me for a dog, the man who knew me from head to toe—and yet, nothing at all.

He wore black. Of course. Always so dramatic. Tailored suit. Gold Rolex. Eyes that once made me soft now only made my rage sharper. And yet, he paused. The moment he saw my eyes, everything about his confident stride wavered for half a second.

Admiration. Pure. Undeniable.

In his eyes, I wasn't just beautiful—I was divine. A vision in emerald silk and victory, a goddess resurrected from her own ashes.

His lips twitched. Not quite a smile. Something else. Longing. Or maybe hatred or admiration.

And I let him look. Let him drink it in. Let him feel the full impact of what slits, cleavage and vengeance.

Because he will beg. But not now. Not yet.

"Catherine," he said slowly, as he slid into the seat opposite mine. "I heard a mother of three girls was haunting my casino tonight."

"Not haunting," I replied, tracing a finger over the rim of my wine glass. "Just collecting something for diapers and milk, you know they are now very expensive..."

Jhing Jhing and Mylene sat behind me, quiet but alert. They knew the stakes were more than just money. This was personal. The kind of battle that only looked polite on the surface. Underneath, it was blood and betrayal.

The dealer shuffled.

Alec leaned forward; eyes narrowed. "One million. Winner takes all. No splits."

"Deal," I said. I forced a grin, even though my insides were anything but steady.

Mick stood nearby, watching. The crowd hushed. Even the slot machines seemed to quiet, like the whole casino held its breath.

First Hand.

I let Alec win it. On purpose.

Let him feel confident.

I didn't know if I could stand from the soft chair without falling later, without me wanting to stab him with my shoe. Everything felt off—my mouth muscles sore from being smiling for so long, my stomach weak from hunger.

He smirked. His ego inflated like a parade balloon.

Second hand? I crushed him. A straight flush.

Whispers started. Someone gasped. Alec narrowed his eyes. Not used to losing.

Third hand. Bluff. A bluff so good, I almost believed myself. He folded. I took the pot. More gasps.

The high roller floor turned into a theatre. We were the stars. But only one of us had read the script. He stared at me across the green felt, jaw tense. I could feel it—the tension rising under his skin. The disbelief.

And then the desire. Oh, he wanted me. This body. This mind. This fire.

God, I was so damn hot.

He licked his lips once.

Quick. Subtle. But I saw it. His fingers twitched over his chips. He leaned forward. "What do you want from me, Catherine with three kids?"

"To play," I purred. "One last hand. All or nothing."

The room went still.

Mylene grabbed my arm. "Cathy—don't. Please. This is too much. My eye lashes can't handle this."

"I know what I'm doing," I whispered.

Final Hand.

The cards came down.

My pulse slowed. Focus honed. I remembered the code. The flaws I installed. The RFID system. The vibrational alerts under my ring. The dealer was mine. The casino was mine. Alec thought it was his.

Wrong.

He played aggressively. He had to. His empire was crumbling. He had Chinese, Korean and Yakuza troubles, traitors, money bleeding from every wall.

And now, I was stealing his soul in public.

"Showdown," the dealer announced.

He revealed his hand.

Full House.

He smirked.

I revealed mine.

Royal Flush.

Gasps. Screams. A woman fainted in the corner. Someone dropped their martini. Cameras flashed. Security stiffened.

Alec stared. His eyes didn't move from my face.

His frown deepened as if he'd somehow read my thoughts.

Whatever he saw didn't please him.

Because, boy, my very presence commanded authority.

My body was a weapon—powerful, timeless. Every sweet plum muscle, every movement, imbued with delicate feminine strength.

I know it was overwhelming for him, as though the very air around me shifted with my power. Ha! That was the power of soft plump, cute overlapping curves, defined waist and fuller hips, asshole.

"Impossible," he whispered.

Impossible my ass. You're nothing but a second rate trying hard pathetic copycat.

Of course, for added drama, I stood slowly, letting the slit of my dress reveal just enough to make him lose what little logic he had left.

These curves could start a war, dick head.

"Nothing's impossible," I said. "Not when I build the house."

I turned.

He reached for my arm.

"Who are you?"

I looked back and dramatically sighed, shifting my weight against the table.

His eyes—desperate. Hungry. Destroyed.

"You want me," I said softly. "But you can't afford me." And with that, I walked out. Chips in hand. Dignity intact. A million pounds richer. And dayyymn! It felt amazing. I never thought watching those cringe-worthy-teenage-dramas on Netflix was indeed a great help. But most importantly?

One step closer to revenge.

Chapter 14

The next morning was... war.

I woke up with my face half-buried in an empty bag of tortilla chips, the sharp crunch stabbing into my cheekbone like regret and wet-dirty wipes. My head was pounding so hard I thought maybe someone had set off a tiny marching band inside my skull—complete with cymbals and war drums.

There were glittery false lashes stuck to the side of the coffee table. One of my high heels was wedged into a potted plant.

And the unmistakable scent of regret and expensive perfume clung to the air like bad karma.

"Ugh…" I groaned, sitting up slowly. Big mistake. The world tilted.

Jhing Jhing was sprawled across the couch like a broken action figure, one leg thrown over the armrest, her dress riding up halfway to her ribs. She had a feather boa around her neck like a battle trophy and one eyelash hanging on for dear life.

Her phone buzzed under her thigh.

Mylene? Poor woman was curled in foetal position under the dining table, murmuring something that sounded like, "Never trust a man with a fake nose and blue necktie…"

Wine bottles were scattered like battlefield casualties.

Empty. Some half-full.

One still sitting in the ice bucket we clearly forgot about halfway through our impromptu celebration. Lipstick marks on every glass, every corner, and somehow—somehow—one kiss print on the television screen.

And then… the audience.

Seven children. Our children. Three of mine, two of Jhing Jhing and a twin of Mylene. All in pink pyjamas. Standing in judgmental silence.

Maya was glaring at me, her arms crossed and a dishtowel on her shoulder like a disapproving aunt. "Mom, you look like you wrestled a raccoon. And lost."

Jaya, my baby, was latched onto my boob like she was recharging her soul.

Didn't care about my sins, just wanted her breakfast.

Aliya? She was sitting on the floor, picking chips off the carpet like it was treasure. "Mmm, salty!"

Jhing Jhing's kids were whispering to each other, holding up Mylene's phone and snapping photos of the "crime scene" like little detectives.

Mylene's twins? Angels. Except for the part where they tied socks around the dog's ears and declared him King of Hangover Hill.

Three babysitters stood in the kitchen, dressed in crisp uniforms, flipping pancakes and pouring orange juice with faces as blank and calm as assassins.

They said nothing. Not a single word.

But the judgment… oh, it hung in the air like cigar smoke.

Thick. Inescapable.

"Good morning, ma'am," one of them said, her tone neutral. "Would you like some aspirin with your scrambled eggs?"

"Yes," I croaked, pulling a Dorito out of my bra. "And maybe a new liver."

"Coming right up."

Mylene rolled out from under the table with a groan. "Why does my tongue taste like rotten durian and floor cleaner?"

Jhing Jhing lifted her head from the couch, blinking at the ceiling. "Did we… won last night?"

I blinked, trying to recall.

Oh yes. We *did* win.

One million pounds, a scandal, and Alec's frozen, love-struck face across the poker table. Oh, we *won*.

"I think," I said slowly, cradling Jaya with one arm, "we might have broken the entire system."

Maya sighed, holding up a newspaper that one of the babysitters had neatly folded on the kitchen counter. The headline screamed:

"Mystery Woman Strikes Again: High Stakes, High Drama, and a Slap Heard Across the Casino."

There was a blurry photo of me standing triumphant with chips in hand, Alec in the background looking like he'd seen a ghost and fallen in love at the same time.

"Explain," Maya said, deadpan.

"I'm... investing," I said. "In your future."

Jhing Jhing laughed so hard she nearly fell off the couch.

Mylene groaned. "We need to burn these dresses. And my heels. And maybe our fingerprints."

Aliya climbed up beside me and offered me a soggy chip. "You are a good mommy."

I nearly cried.

Me the assassin, the kingpin. She called me good.

"Okay," I said, hugging both Jaya and Aliya tightly, "no more wine-fuelled revenge poker nights."

Everyone looked at me.

I paused.

"...on weekdays," I added.

The babysitter slid a plate of eggs and aspirin in front of me. The smell almost killed me. But damn, victory had never tasted so greasy and glorious.

And as the girls giggled and the kids slowly began to run around in their usual chaotic fashion, I realized something powerful...

This mess? This was mine. And I was winning.

One scandal at a time.

*****

The next morning, the city was still wet with last night's rain, the streets shimmering like they'd been scrubbed clean of sin. The air was crisp, sharp in a way that felt like it could slice through all the mistakes of the night before. I walked up the stairs to Jhing Jhing's flat with purpose, a warm cup of overpriced matcha in one hand and a sealed Manila envelope in the other. Inside was three hundred thousand pounds. Neatly packed. Freshly transferred. Clean as a whistle.

I knocked.

Twice.

Loud enough to wake the dead, but soft enough not to startle her kids.

The door creaked open after a few seconds, revealing a wild-haired, half-awake Jhing in her pink panda pyjamas, blinking at me like I'd risen from a coffin.

"Cathy—what the hell? It's barely eight and I swear if you came to borrow my last pancake, I will throw you off the—"

I handed her the envelope.

She paused. Her fingers took it before her brain even registered what was happening. She opened it slowly, the way you open a letter bomb or a wedding invite from an ex.

Her mouth dropped open. "Is this... Is this real?"

"As real as your hangover," I said, sipping my matcha. "You deserve it. We all do."

Her knees buckled slightly, and she leaned against the door frame, blinking fast. "What the f—Catherine. This is—this is three hundred thousand pounds."

"Yeah," I said. "I will give the same to Mylene. Twenty grand each to the babysitters. They handled chaos like they were paid by MI6."

She stared at me like she was trying to find the hidden camera. "What is this? A prank? A reverse pyramid scheme? Are you dying? Are we dying?"

I smirked. "No. Not yet. I just… felt like sharing." I've totalled all our winning within two nights and it was almost 1.3 million pounds.

Jhing stepped forward and hugged me so tight I dropped my cup. "You insane bitch," she whispered. "You're insane. But you're my favourite kind of insane."

We stood there for a minute. Her gratitude wasn't loud. It was quiet, trembling. It came with soft hiccups and a tightened grip. I could feel it in the way her shoulders shook slightly, like she hadn't exhaled properly in years.

Next stop: Mylene.

She didn't scream when I showed up. She just stared at the envelope in her lap like it had appeared from the clouds. Her twins were playing in the living room behind her, giggling over cartoons, unaware that life had just taken a sharp, better turn for their mama.

Her eyes were wet.

"I was going to sell my necklace," she said softly, still staring at the bills. "The one my mother gave me. Just to pay rent. And now…"

She didn't finish. She didn't need to.

Instead, she reached out and grabbed my hand with both of hers. "Thank you. Thank you, Catherine.

For everything.

For not making me feel small when I was drowning."

I nodded, words caught somewhere between my throat and pride.

I didn't tell them about the rest. That the remaining money went to an orphanage just down the road from the casino. That I stood in front of their cracked windows and watched little kids burst into laughter when the volunteers told them they'd have enough money now for beds, food, books, new shoes. That one tiny girl with hair like ink ran up and hugged my knees and called me "Santa with eyeliner."

That part was just for me.

Because that morning, I felt something different. Something I hadn't felt in years, maybe lifetimes. It wasn't adrenaline. It wasn't vengeance. It wasn't the quiet satisfaction of a plan going perfectly.

It was happiness.

Raw. Loud. Stupid, sun-kissed happiness that bloomed in my chest and made everything feel brand new. Even in the middle of chaos, surrounded by shrieking children and bad breath and mismatched pyjamas, I felt it.

Joy.

Mylene, Jhing Jhing, and I sat later in my living room with mugs of tea and leftover pastries from the babysitters' breakfast stash. We didn't talk about Alec. Or the casino. Or what came next.

We just sat. We laughed. We teased each other.

We were no longer just survivors.

We were sisters-in-arms.

Battle-tested. Lipstick-stained. Broke-then-blessed. I'd shared the spoils of war not because I had to, but because it was right. Because they deserved to win too. Because even assassins need family.

And these women?

These fierce, funny, ridiculous women?

They were mine.

After yet another small breakfast party at my living room, the sun was finally creeping higher now, casting golden bars of light through the sheer curtains, dancing across our cluttered chaos of a living room. Jhing Jhing had her hair up in a pineapple bun, Mylene was curled into a blanket that had once been draped across my couch like a throw, and I—Leon, the reluctant assassin in borrowed flesh—was sitting barefoot on the floor in pink Barbie sweatpants, letting a toddler use my back as a jungle gym.

The money had changed something. Not just bank

accounts. Not just bills.

It changed us. It softened something brittle inside all three of us. For years, Catherine, and Jhing Jhing, they'd fought. Fought for food, fought for rent, fought for time, for peace, for themselves. And now, for the first time, they were breathing differently. It wasn't desperation. It wasn't survival mode. It was something else. I felt it too. I felt the ease in my mind. I felt how grateful Catherine was. To the new her.

"I'm going to buy an air fryer and a new washing machine that talks," Jhing Jhing said dreamily, flipping through her phone. "And a knock knock fridge. A fancy one. The one with twelve presets. I don't even know what a preset is, but I want it."

Mylene laughed, her head leaning against my shoulder. "I'm going to buy a day off. Just one whole day. I'm going to rent a hotel room and sleep without a baby crawling up my nose."

I looked between the two of them. "You both dream so small."

"Oh please," Jhing Jhing snorted. "What would you do, Mrs. Secret Millions? Build a bat cave?"

"Already did," I muttered under my breath, then smirked when they stared.

Aliya wandered in with chip crumbs still stuck to her pyjamas and a shoe that wasn't hers. She climbed into Mylene's lap, looked around, and declared with utmost toddler authority: "This house messy."

We all burst into laughter.

And in the middle of that joy—raw, stupid, pure—I knew something deeper had happened.

They weren't just my co-conspirators anymore. They weren't just my excuses for returning to the light.

They were my anchors.

Mylene, who despite her chaos and twin tornadoes, had the sharpest instincts and deepest empathy I'd ever seen in a woman.

Jhing Jhing, whose mouth could cut a man in half but whose heart was already divided amongst all of us in equal slices.

We had lived lives that most people couldn't even fathom. They didn't know about the tears we cried alone in kitchens, or the way we held our babies tighter when the world tried to split us apart. They didn't know about the nights we went hungry just to save one more bill, or the fear of a knock on the door that wasn't friendly.

But now?

Now we had power.

Real power.

Because we weren't alone anymore.

And even as I plotted my next move against Alec—even as I imagined the way he would fall, how I would carve justice from his bones—I knew the war I was truly fighting was to protect this.

This tiny little sanctuary.

This fortress of fierce women and sticky toddlers and air fryer dreams.

Chapter 15

Later that afternoon, the doorbell rang. It was the courier with the receipts for the orphanage donation. I didn't let anyone else see it. I signed for it, tucked it away in the safe beneath the fake floor panel in my bedroom.

And I smiled.

Because yes, I was still a weapon. Still death in lipstick. Still vengeance on heels.

But now?

I was also a provider. A protector. A giver.

A mother. A friend. And one day, when Alec was lying broken beneath everything he tried to destroy, he would finally understand what made me powerful wasn't just the secrets I kept or the systems I rigged.

It was *them*. My girls. My sisters. My chaos. My family.

The night was thick with tension. Alec's office was a fortress of glass and steel, overlooking the neon heartbeat of the city, but inside, the atmosphere was anything but calm. Papers were scattered, digital files flashed across multiple screens, and a few of his closest men poured over every detail they could find about me—about *Catherine*.

They dug deep.

They found Ray, the husband who was more of a liability than an asset—his half a million-pound loss at the casino practically screaming failure. They found Jhing Jhing and Mylene—nice enough women, but nothing particularly suspicious. No criminal records, no dangerous connections. Just everyday chaos and a few messy lives tangled with mine.

But *me*? Catherine? She was cleaned. Nothing even remotely suspicious and I am Leon Darrow for a reason. I play pink Peppa Pig poker for breakfast and eat alphabet cereal.

Now…Only a ghost in their system. Just an ant lost in the belly of vipers.

And Alec? He snarled through gritted teeth, frustrated as the trail kept going cold. What he didn't know was that the woman he thought he could trace was smart enough not to leave a trace that could implicate me. Catherine, the extra-large tired mother of three was replaced by *me*—Leon Darrow, the unstoppable storm beneath the calm.

Across the city, I sat in my high-tech lair beneath the garage. Joe Smith's voice crackled through the encrypted line.

"Alec's onto the missing shipment to Dubai. Chinese and Koreans are calling it quits. He's pissed. Desperate even. Wants blood."

I smiled, fingers tapping the edge of the sleek, military-grade table.

"Let him come."

Joe chuckled. "You're playing a dangerous game, girl."

"I'm not playing. I'm winning."

Japan had already bowed, their underground factions bending to my will through strategy and silent threats. Alec's empire was cracking, and his panic was evident—his men turning on each other, whispers of traitors hiding in the shadows.

Meanwhile, Dorothy had slipped away, tired of the chaos, leaving Alec with nothing but his crumbling pride and a half-empty wine bottle.

The city didn't know it yet, but the kingpin was changing.

And tonight? Alec would bleed in ways he never imagined.

My vengeance wasn't a spark—it was a wildfire, and it was just getting started.

Few weeks later.

The grocery bags were heavier than they should've been, or maybe it was just the fact that my arms were full with more than produce—I had three sugar-loaded girls bouncing around me like untamed circus performers. Maya was jabbering a mile a minute about how the cotton candy "melted like clouds in her mouth," while Aliya sang loudly (and off-key) the jingle from a cereal box. The baby was strapped to my chest, kicking like a wild pony, her mouth sticky from the pink ice cream I swore I wouldn't give her—but gave anyway, because motherhood is just saying *yes* when you're too tired to say *no*.

It was chaos. Pure, loud, sparkly chaos.

And then we passed it.

The Tux Shop.

Not just any tux shop. It was sleek, modern, and almost too clean for a place that dealt with secrets deadlier than a bullet. A velvet front for the information ring I helped set up during my college days—when I wasn't juggling illegal arms, assassinations, and political coups. Those were simpler times, really.

Behind the velvet curtains and the glass shelves of imported Italian bowties was a backroom that traded intel like stocks. My friend, Lucas, ran it now—ever the quiet fox, too smart for his own good and too discreet for Alec to ignore.

That's why Alec was there.

I saw him before he saw me.

He stood near the counter, trying on an ash-grey jacket that hugged his broad shoulders too perfectly. His dark hair was slicked back, jaw tight, and that permanent scowl etched between his brows. He was talking to the salesman, but I knew better. His sharp eyes scanned the mirrors, the surroundings—always calculating.

I could've walked away. I should've walked away.

Instead, I pulled the hood of my oversized jumper lower, grabbed a boring blue necktie from the nearest stand, and strutted in like I belonged. My trainers squeaked against the marble floors. My girls followed behind like drunken ducklings, one tripping over her laces, another still licking a lolly, and the baby pulling at my hoodie string like it was her personal swing.

Alec turned.

At first, there was nothing. No flicker of recognition. Just another man bored of women, glancing over with disinterest.

Then came the second look.

And the third.

I saw the flicker. Confusion. Familiarity. That ghost of memory clawing at the edge of his mind.

He tilted his head, those steel-blue eyes narrowing as he spoke my name with the kind of disbelief that made me want to laugh. "Catherine?"

"Don't look so surprised," I said, waving the necktie lazily like I was genuinely considering it for Ray—the man I could legally murder if the courts allowed.

Alec's lip twitched. Not a smile. But something.

"You look... different."

"Yeah," I said, glancing down at my outfit: hoodie, leggings, baby carrier, and a chocolate stain on my shoulder. "Motherhood looks good on me."

He scoffed, voice low and dry. "You? You're just a bug. A bug that made me think… you were something else."

I bit the inside of my cheek to keep from laughing. There it was. The insult. The bait. But his eyes told another story.

They lingered.

Too long.

They traced the curve of my cheekbone, even without makeup. They scanned my lips, the slope of my neck, the easy way I handled chaos while juggling two shopping bags and a teething baby.

He was intrigued.

And irritated by it.

I knew men like Alec. I used to train them. Command them. Kill them. He was the kind that hated being curious about someone he couldn't control.

Good.

"Coffee?" I said casually, like I wasn't about to blow his entire life apart.

He hesitated.

The salesman cleared his throat awkwardly. My baby let out a tiny fart. One of my girls dropped her half-eaten donut and started crying like the world had ended.

I stood there smiling.

"Seriously?" Alec said, almost laughing. "You want coffee?"

"You're the one loitering in a shop I dream to build, wearing a jacket too tight for your ego. You owe me at least a latte."

He blinked. Then—of course—he said yes.

Because I knew how to bait a man like Alec. Not with cleavage or lipstick, but with something far more dangerous.

My mind. And so, we walked. Me, in my grocery-stained hoodie.

Him, in his designer suit.

And behind us, my three girls skipping like manic fairies, giggling as they pulled on the back of Alec's jacket.

I smiled like a woman who wasn't about to destroy him.

But deep down? Leon Darrow—the real me—was sharpening his blade.

The moment I stepped into the café with the kids in tow, Alec already seated by the window, his profile sharp against the morning sunlight. He looked like a painting—expensive, calculated, too clean for the real world. The kind of man who should be sipping scotch in a penthouse, not waiting for a woman like me—hoodie, sneakers, a baby on my hip, and two toddlers dragging jelly-covered fingers across the glass door.

He looked up. And I saw it. That flicker in his eyes.

Not recognition—he already knew who I was. No. It was fascination. Curiosity.

He couldn't understand it. Couldn't place me.

How a woman like this, in a mess of children and cheap clothes, had walked into his casino like she owned the building. How she had wiped the floor with the high rollers. How she had laughed with two loud friends and winked at the dealer while sweeping millions off his felt-covered table.

I crossed the table with the chaos trailing behind me like ribbons in a war parade. Maya was humming loudly. Aliya kept pointing at a croissant display like it owed her money. The baby had fallen asleep but was drooling across my shoulder like a tiny drunk pirate.

He didn't say anything at first.

Just stared.

I dropped the diaper bag with a soft thud, grabbed the extra chair with one foot, and settled into the seat like a woman with nothing to prove and everything to hide.

"You look like hell," Alec said finally, lips curled in something that almost passed for amusement.

"Thanks. It's my new scent—Eau de Breast Milk and Cookie Crumbs."

One of the toddlers squealed in the background. Something broke—probably a ceramic plate. The barista gasped. I didn't even flinch.

He stared at the children. "They're yours."

"Congratulations, you can count."

"And Ray's."

I let my eyes roll lazily toward him. "You bring him up like he matters."

Alec tilted his head. I could see him trying to read me, dig through the layers—peel back. But I was better. Always had been.

"Ray, your husband. He gambled away everything," he said. "Then you won it all back. Funny how that worked out."

I smiled like I was tired of life. Like I was just a woman barely holding it together. "You know what's funnier? I thought being a good wife meant standing by him. Turns out, it just meant standing in quicksand."

His jaw clenched.

I had him.

He was curious. He wasn't here just to confirm suspicions. He wanted to know how I did it. How I played him. How I rigged the table right under his smug nose. How I knew the drop points, the inside dealers, the weaknesses he thought were buried.

But I wasn't giving him anything. Not yet.

Instead, I sipped my coffee and leaned in just a little. "You ever feel like you're with the wrong person, Alec?"

He narrowed his eyes. "You trying to flirt with me now?"

I gave him a tired laugh. "Don't flatter yourself. I just want to remember what it feels like to sit across a man who actually uses his brain."

Aliya threw a sugar packet at Maya. The baby burped like a monster. A cup of orange juice tipped over and started dripping off the edge of the table.

Alec ignored the mess like it didn't exist. His focus was locked on me. Unblinking.

"You're not what you seem."

"Neither are you."

He hesitated. Then: "I know someone's bleeding me dry. The Dubai shipment. The missing funds. The winning tables. You know something?"

I frowned. "I also know how to make homemade baby wipes out of paper towels and aloe vera. Doesn't mean I know everything that is happening on earth. I couldn't even have a five-hour decent sleep let alone a ship in Dubai."

"Hmmm?"

Of course he was prying for information, God. He was desperate.

How naive.

We sat there, staring. My fingers danced around the rim of my mug.

His were steepled under his chin, elbows on the table.

He was playing chess.

I was playing poker. Two games, one board.

Finally, I said with a sigh, "I'm tired, Alec. I've got three kids, a husband who keeps chasing dice, and a laundry pile taller than your ego. Maybe I just want someone to talk to."

He didn't believe me. Not for a second.

My instincts screamed at me to breathe deeper, to soak up more of him, for me to remember how he betrayed me, but I fought it. I had to stay in control. The tension between us was palpable, thick with unspoken words, yet all I could do was stand there and try not to crumble under his gaze.

But that didn't stop him from leaning back and relaxing just a little. He liked it. Liked the idea of being the one I confided in. The man who saw through the tired mother act. The man who maybe—just maybe—could win me over.

Let him think it.

Let him want it.

Let him sit across from me every morning until he begged for a glimpse of the woman beneath the chaos. The goddess wrapped in spit-up and cracker crumbs. The mastermind playing him like a cello.

Leon Darrow was dead.

Catherine? She was just a mother in sweatpants. But whatever I was now—

Alec wanted it. And he didn't even know that by sipping coffee with me…

…he'd already lost.

Chapter 16

The sun was already beginning to dip behind the skyline as I loaded the kids into the SUV—Aliya with her chip crumbs, Maya with her sticky fingers clutching an empty candy wrapper, and my baby with that distant, milk-drunk expression. All three were asleep within minutes, mouths open, little heads tilted at odd angles in their car seats.

Peaceful. Beautiful.

But me?

I wasn't peaceful. Not when I caught the glint of a black car in my rearview mirror. Not when it took every same turn I did—two rights, a long detour into the quieter part of the city, and still it followed. Like a shadow with tinted windows.

Alec.

Of course it was him.

I smirked to myself. So, the café chat did rattle him. He wasn't done with me. Not by a long shot. He probably sent one of his men, one of those quiet, sharp-jawed drivers with earpieces and false passports. And if he was watching me, tailing me… then I might as well make the show worth it.

An idea bloomed in my head.

Delicious. Dramatic. Deadly charming.

I reached into the glove compartment and pulled out the small burner phone I hadn't used in weeks. Joe picked up before the second ring.

"Boss?"

"It's me."

There was a pause. Then a slightly amused, "You never call me on this one unless it's stupid or genius."

"Both. I need you to remotely access the SUV's control board. Just enough to fry the ignition module. Disable the brakes."

A low whistle from the other end. "You've got your kids in the car."

"I'm Leon Darrow's girl, remember? You think I'd let them get hurt?" I smiled at the snoring trio in the back. "Just give me a light scare. I want Alec to think I'm in trouble."

"You're playing the damsel?"

"I'm reinventing the genre. Call it strategic distress."

He laughed, then I heard fingers flying over keys. "Ten seconds after your signal, it'll glitch. You'll lose brakes and steering for roughly fifteen seconds before I re-route it to backup. Long enough?"

"More than enough. Let's make Alec's heart skip a beat."

I ended the call.

Pulled the SUV into the slower lanes of traffic near the bridge. The river shimmered below. I took a deep breath, tightened my grip on the steering wheel, and whispered, "Showtime."

Three blocks later, I tapped the signal light three times.

Ten seconds.

The SUV shuddered.

"Mommy?" Maya mumbled, eyes fluttering open.

The dashboard lights blinked, one after another. Power steering froze. My foot hit the brake—nothing.

"Okay, okay…" I muttered, swerving the wheel hard, letting the heavy body of the car veer toward the shoulder.

The kids screamed. The baby wailed.

Aliya was yelling, "MOMMY WE'RE DYING!"

"No, baby, we're fine, it's just—AHHH!"

I added the scream for theatrical flair. Even reached into the glove compartment and flung a pile of receipts to make it more chaotic. I jerked the wheel again and let the SUV bump hard into a low metal guardrail with a thud that made the girls wail louder.

The black car behind us screeched to a stop.

A second later, Alec emerged.

Not one of his men.

Him.

Of course he would come himself.

He was already at my door before I even finished pretending to breathe heavy. He pulled it open, face pale, eyes wide with something dangerously close to panic.

"Catherine!"

He said it like he meant it. Not like a name. Like a prayer.

Before I could even react, he squatted beside me. Not in front of me, where he'd block any chance of escape, but off to the side. It was a subtle movement, one that showed how thoroughly he had already sized up the situation. He didn't underestimate me. I appreciated that.

Chapter 17

"I—I don't know what happened!" I stammered, letting my hands shake just enough. "I couldn't brake, the wheel just—just locked!"

He crouched beside me like some tailored superhero, ignoring the bloodcurdling cries from my backseat.

Sure, I noted that I would buy them minted ice cream later.

His hands gripped my shoulders. "Are you okay? Are they okay?"

I nodded, breathless. "They're scared, but we're okay. Just… shaken."

"I'm calling someone. I'll have the car towed and a team sent—"

"No," I cut in quickly, grabbing his wrist with trembling fingers. "Please don't make this into a thing. I just want to get them home."

His expression softened. I saw it. The shift. The moment the predator became the protector. My mess of a face, no makeup, hair tied in a lopsided bun, three kids wailing in the back—and he still looked at me like I was a mystery he hadn't solved.

And oh, he wanted to.

I let a tear roll down. Just one. Just enough. "I'm trying so hard," I whispered. "And everything just keeps falling apart. First Ray, now this. I just want to feel safe again."

He swallowed hard. "You will," he said, his voice cutting through the tension. It was low, sharp as ice, brittle with a coldness that sent a shiver down my spine. His gaze flicked from my eyes, down to my throat—like he was considering something.

I pressed the advantage. "Will you… can you drive us home?"

He didn't hesitate.

"I'll follow you in my car. Transfer the kids over."

And that's how I ended up in the front passenger seat of Alec's expensive black sedan, with Maya and Aliya passed out in the back beside their baby sibling, safely tucked in after the drama. Alec drove like he was carrying precious glass.

His jaw tight. His hands steady. But his mind? Oh, it was racing.

And me? I leaned my head against the window, looking small, vulnerable.

A mother of three. A woman scorned. A victim of bad luck.

A siren cloaked in motherhood. I knew exactly what I was doing.

And Alec? He had no idea what storm he was inviting into his heart. Or his kingdom.

After a small talk to the patrol huge policeman with a belly of a mother, Alec's black sedan purred quietly along the damp street, the city lights glinting against the raindrops that still clung to the windows. I sat in the passenger seat, my back straight, arms wrapped protectively around a sleeping Aliya, while Jaya leaned against the opposite door, snoring softly, her little legs tangled in the seatbelt.

The silence in the car was thick but not uncomfortable. It was the kind of silence that made you think—reflect. Alec's fingers tapped softly on the steering wheel; his eyes trained on the road ahead. He hadn't said much since we left the hospital. Just quiet glances and the occasional clearing of his throat, like he had more to say but couldn't find the words.

"We're close," he said finally, voice low, warm, steady. He radiated a danger so intense, I felt it pressing against my chest. Anyone dumb enough to stand between us in that moment would be torn apart in a heartbeat. Of course, I play the scared mother with boobs so big I swore it would ruin my bra…correction, new extra super bra.

I shifted a little in my seat. "You can just drop us near the bus stop. We'll walk from there." I murmured with the tiredness voice I could muster. If I stayed here, pretending to be weak, smart and a goddess at the same time he'd keep looking at me like I was some fragile thing. I need to let him think that.

He blinked, turning slightly toward me. "What?"

"I said—"

"I heard you," he cut in, a little incredulous. "But I'm not dropping you at a bus stop, Catherine. You've got three kids with you. It's cold. It's dark. And you're still shaken up from the accident."

I sighed. "I'm fine. We're fine."

God, I never thought there would be time in my life that I would act like a damsel in distress, and boy, I enjoyed every minute of this. Somehow, Catherine, this body wanted to be one, for once in her life, she wanted to be the damsel saved by the knight in shining armour.

"I'm fine, really." I purred, my voice light, teasing yet, wanting. But inside, my heart raced. Raced to just want to stab the bastard until his blood scattered on the wet dirty street, "I mean... I don't want to—" The last word slipped from my mouth awkwardly, a squeak I couldn't control. Great. Just great. Is this what it felt like to be fucking damsel? I quickly smothered the urge to bolt for the non-existent exit.

"I didn't ask if you were fine. I said I'm taking you home." His expression hardened, a dark scowl painting his features. I couldn't help but feel a flicker of sympathy for him—ha! what a load of bollocks, I pretended to think that he was terrifying, but that scowl? It would keep even the bravest of women at arm's length.

And where would that leave me? Alone with him. Trapped in a cage with the embodiment of power.

There! I got you assh*le.

"Please Catherine," His tone wasn't angry. It was firm, unyielding—like the voice of someone who'd already made the decision before asking. I opened my mouth to argue but stopped. He was doing it to show off. He was doing it to control me.

He was doing it because—despite everything—he cared?

What bullcraaap! Of course, I know he thought he could have me under his palm by acting like a knight in fucking bullshit.

A few minutes later, he pulled into the familiar corner by my building. The old apartment complex stood like a weary soldier, its peeling paint and flickering porch light somehow comforting in its constancy. He shifted the gear into park and turned toward me.

"Let me carry her," he offered gently, reaching toward Jaya.

Hell no! Not my kid.

Catherine's kid?

NO!

I shook my head, for once I wanted to show him, I am just a mere weak mother of three chaos. I bit my lip so hard and continued the momentary ploy.

But hell! Play it cool, Leon, I told myself. Don't let him see how angry you are. I shook my head quickly, instinctively tightening my arms around her. "No, I got it," I said. "She's lighter than she looks."

He paused, then nodded, pulling his hand back slowly.

I leaned over and gently nudged Jaya then to the two girls, "Baby, wake up. We're home."

Maya and Aliya groaned, their tiny eyelids fluttered open, dazed and confused, but Jaya yawned and looped her arms around my neck without protest. I grabbed Aliya's hand, and motioned to Maya to follow me without questions and she followed sleepily, dragging her backpack behind her.

Before I stepped out, I turned to Alec, my voice softer now.

"Thank you," I said. "I know we don't talk like... like normal people do. But I mean it. You showing up after the accident—being there—I'll never forget that."

A tiny rebellion against the weight of this moment. The silence between us was thick, charged, like the air before a storm. He shot me another look—harder this time, but still that unsettling calm and overconfident smirk like I owed him the fucking universe. His gaze met mine, dark and unreadable.

"You don't need to thank me."

No, I don't. I need to kill you. Just you wait!

"I am after all your knight in shining armour," he continued, as though the matter were settled.

THE F*CKING NERVE!

Chapter 18

"Thank you, I need that," I replied with the weakest, fakest longing voice I could muster. "You didn't have to come. But you did. And the girls… we needed someone. You were that someone."

He was quiet for a beat. Then his hand went to the gear again. "I'll call my guy first thing in the morning. We'll get your SUV sorted. Towed. Repaired. You'll have it back soon. I have a team of the finest mechanics in the world, twiddling their thumbs, waiting for the moment to strike."

I blinked, a little stunned.

"You really don't have to—"

"I know," he said, cutting me off with a small smile. "But I want to—" He paused, the silence stretching between us thick with unsaid things. When he looked at me again, his gaze was intense, searching. I could almost taste his needs. It wasn't a casual inspection—it was something else, something I couldn't fully place. But it made my skin burn off more hatred that I didn't know existed, and my breath hitched in my chest because I didn't want anything in this world but to kill him.

"And I couldn't help myself but to help you." He continued with the intensity of a liar. Not from love, not from romance—no. But from the simple truth that sometimes, in a world of liars and wolves, someone still showed up when it counted.

That left me a little breathless. Jesus. This man could make any woman forget how to breathe without even touching her. Ha! If I was just Catherine, but no. I am LEON the destroyer. His own fucking brother.

I breathed harder this time and nodded, adjusted Jaya against my shoulder, and gave him a look I hadn't given anyone in years.

Not trust.

But… something close.

Then I stepped out into the crisp night air, my shoes clicking against the wet pavement, the smell of damp concrete and distant barbecue drifting through the alley. Aliya ran ahead, laughing quietly to herself, her energy restored by the thought of home.

As I reached the door of the building, I looked back. "Thank you again," I shouted, not sounding as strong as I wanted.

Alec was still there.

Watching.

Waiting.

Like a silent guardian in a luxury sedan. And for the first time in a long time, I didn't feel entirely alone. Because heaven gave me the second chance for revenge.

The door clicked shut behind us. The moment I shut the apartment door behind me with my foot—Jaya still curled against my chest like a warm little pillow—I grinned.

Not the fake smile I used for Ray.

Not the strained, careful one for schoolteachers or grocery clerks. No.

This grin was pure. Ferocious. Delicious.

Because Alec Darrow, my beloved traitor of a brother, had just dropped me and my three chaos goblins off like some shiny white knight behind the wheel of a sedan he probably bought with my old blood money.

Oh, darling. You think I'm your new little toy? Some lonely mother project to help you sleep better at night?

Ha! You have no idea you just invited the lioness back into the den. In heels.

The hallway light flickered like it always did — one final wink from the universe before bedtime chaos. Maya kicked off her sneakers and ran straight for the couch, mumbling something about cartoons. Jaya, now half-awake, clung to my neck with a soft whimper before I gently laid her down on the couch, tucking a pillow under her head. Aliya was already rummaging through the fridge, probably looking for that last juice box she hid behind the broccoli.

And me? I smirked. I stood by the door for a second, my back resting against the cold wood, arms crossed, heart still pounding—not from exhaustion. No. It was thrill.

Pure, electric thrill.

Finally, Alec was in my palm. The bastard really wanted to play the part of my knight in shining armour, huh? Dropping us off like some kind-hearted gentleman, offering help, looking at me with those unreadable eyes like I was some fragile little woman in need of saving.

F*ck him!

I am Leon Darrow. His brother. His blood. The one who took bullets for him. Built his empire's bones. Hid his sins. Killed his enemies. And what did he do?

He repaid me with a kiss on the forehead and my own death sentence—delivered with venom from my pet spider, Blacky. The irony still stung. He used my spider.

I laughed under my breath, shaking my head. If I hadn't entered Catherine body... if my soul hadn't clawed its way into this super plus-sized body of a mother, I don't know if I would've had the strength to enter hell with vengeance still burning inside me.

But here I was. Alive. Again. And this time, I didn't need guns or blades. I had hips, curves, eyeliner, and a grocery bill long enough to choke a politician. I had three beautiful chaos machines I called my children.

And now? I had Alec eating from the palm of my perfectly manicured hand.

Oh, he didn't know it yet. He thought he was in control. Thought he could play the saviour while keeping his hands clean.

Please.

He'll beg for my attention before this is over. He'll crawl for my forgiveness.

I strutted toward the kitchen, passing Aliya who was still mid-juicebox conquest, and pulled open the cabinet to grab a wine glass. Poured myself the cheap red stuff that burned like battery acid but felt like power. I took a sip and let the memories creep in again.

That smirk of his when he leaned on the car door. That fake concern. That perfectly pressed shirt and cologne that reeked of manipulation. He thought Catherine was just some struggling single mom. A damsel.

Oh, sweetie. I'm the dragon, not the damsel.

And I may be in leggings and a "Messy Bun, Coffee Run, Done" t-shirt now, but I'm still the man who once ordered ten men dead over a faulty shipment of diamonds — and then had wine with their widows the next day.

I glanced at the reflection of myself in the kitchen window. The face was different, fuller, softer, lined with years of pain and child-rearing. But the eyes?

The eyes still belonged to Leon.

"Game on, little brother," I whispered, raising the glass in a silent toast. "You should've made sure I stayed dead."

I stood in the doorway of the kitchen, arms crossed, staring at the moonlight streaming through the blinds. My apartment smells like laundry detergent, rotten apples and old rice.

And victory.

Alec thought he could play saviour.

He thought my SUV "accident" was a coincidence.

But I saw the gleam in his eyes today—like he'd just discovered a shiny puzzle piece and didn't know whether to kiss it or crush it.

Let him wonder. Let him feel important.

Because while he holds the steering wheel, I've got my hand on the brake lines. And baby, I designed this road.

Let me remind you, Alec:

I am Leon Darrow. Dead to the world. Reborn in stretch marks, cupcake crumbs, and vengeance.

I once ordered the death of three cartel leaders while sipping espresso in my robe.

Now I sort laundry in the morning and plot your demise by dinner.

Soon, very soon, you'll beg for mercy. And I'll show you how soft mercy can feel—right before I take it away.

Maya screamed from the living room. "Mama! Jaya's peeing on the couch again!"

I rolled my eyes, downed the wine in one go, and marched back into the fray.

Assassin by soul. Mother by circumstance.

Let's see who makes it out alive.

That evening, I couldn't sleep. I was thinking. About what went wrong…

It was storming the night I saved Alec's life ten years ago.

Not the soft, movie kind of storm. No poetic drizzle. It was the kind that split trees, that made concrete look like wet tissue paper.

The kind of storm you could hide gunfire in.

We were in Prague. Neutral ground. I had arranged the meeting myself—Leon Darrow, the name people whispered across borders. The man who could disappear whole supply chains if you looked at him wrong. And Alec? He was my baby brother. New to the game. Still smelled like prep school and luxury soap.

He wasn't ready. Not for the Russians.

We were supposed to broker a deal. Simple arms-for-data trade. But the moment we stepped into the chandelier-lit ballroom, I knew we were being set up. The lighting was too clean. The guards stood too tall. And my instincts? They screamed betrayal.

And they were right.

Alec never saw it coming. One moment he was adjusting his cufflinks, the next, a bullet shattered the wine glass near his head. Chaos erupted. I flipped the table. Covered him. My men returned fire while I dragged Alec by the collar out the back exit.

We lost two men that night. One of them had been with me since I was seventeen.

Alec never said thank you.

In fact, months later, he told our father it was my arrogance that brought the ambush.

That it was my ego that endangered the family.

Father believed him. Of course he did. Alec was clean. Pretty. Easier to control. I was the sword you pulled out for blood, not the one you handed to diplomats.

I was sent to South America after that. Banished, really. To clean up some cartel mess with half the resources I needed.

Meanwhile, Alec rose. Slowly. Quietly. Smiling at cameras. Shaking hands. Becoming the face of our operations in Europe.

That I'd rather run with the wolves than sit at polished tables. But betrayal has a sound.

It sounds like your brother laughing over your coffin.

I found out later Alec had known about the setup in Prague. Had even told the Russians to "scare me."

I told myself I didn't care. I still forgave him because that was what brothers do. They forget and forgive and we start anew. I was indeed stupid. And I hated every moment of it.

He just hadn't counted on me walking out alive.

And when he finally plunged that venom into my neck decade later—using my own loyal pet spider to do it?

That was his coronation.

He became the king.

And I? I became a ghost.

Until now.

Chapter 19

Alec's Pov

"She's lying," I muttered, gripping the leather steering wheel until it creaked beneath my hands. "Bitch!" I hissed, fighting against the primal urge within me. I willed the darkness in my mind to retract, but they remained defiantly extended, a cruel reminder of my hunger, which was intensifying with every passing moment. My muscles cramped, a taut reminder of my desperate need. The hatred, the longing to kill again ate me alive. I wanted her so much that it hurts.

Whore!

But she was a *smart* one. I'll give her that.

The kids were cute. Sweet, even. But Catherine—whatever her real name was—had too many shadows in her eyes for a typical struggling mom. I could almost feel her hatred towards me. Like I owed her the fucking Eifel Tower,

No. No, something was off.

The way she handled herself during the accident. The way she talked to the cops—casual but calculated. Her movements were sharp, trained. Like a warrior, not frantic like most mothers would be.

And tonight, when I offered to carry the little one, she refused—politely, but with precision. Like she didn't want my prints anywhere near her kids.

Like she knew something I didn't.

I watched her walk away from the rearview mirror, holding that child like a warrior goddess. The streetlights bathed her in gold, but I wasn't looking at beauty. I was looking at danger wrapped in a floral print dress and pink mom jeans.

Damn it! I want her so bad. She entertained me, and the need to sated the darkness in me echoed my very being. And I didn't want to stop. She was something I wanted. It was intoxicating, like a child tasting candy for the first time and unable to let go of the sweetness. Her smart ass, plum breast, defined curves thrummed through me, filling the hollowness inside, and I hungered for more; I craved it like a drug.

My grip on my sanity tightened as my need to dig deeper.

A part of me still remembered Leon. My brother. My blood. My monster. I killed him because the darkness said so. The darkness wanted his blood. And I did it and boy it was wonderful, grand even! That feeling of greatness feeds my sanity.

Leon…. Leon. Brother. He used to say things like "You either hunt or get hunted, baby brother."

And now, the hunter was gone.

Or was he?

I looked at my phone. Mick had texted twice. No name. Just a number, a photo, and the words:

"Catherine knows how to count cards. Cleaned almost £1.3 million in two nights. But she didn't take a single penny. She gave it all away. Want me to follow?"

I stared at the photo of Catherine. Or whatever she called herself.

She was laughing in the frame—head tilted, eyes glittering like knives. Two other women beside her. Champagne flutes. Glamorous dresses. But it was her expression that twisted something in my gut. That wasn't the face of a desperate woman blowing lottery winnings.

That was a shark circling in silk.

I tapped a voice memo. "Don't follow her yet. Watch from a distance. Find everything. Who she talks to. What she buys. Every bank transaction."

I paused. Then added: "And Mick... don't underestimate her."

That same night, Alec swore to have her...but he would never underestimate her, because just like Leon, she was a force not to be reckoned with.

They were almost identical. He couldn't read her at all. And just like that, just like what happened in the past. It still kills him...He was the prey, always the prey.

Alec was fifteen when he first learned what it meant to be invisible.

It wasn't like in the books, where invisibility granted power, mystery, or escape. No. Alec's version of it was raw, humiliating, soul-cutting nothingness. He was the wallpaper. The shadow behind the golden boy. The second Darrow.

And Leon—oh, Leon—he had everything.

The girls fawned over him, their eyes lighting up like firecrackers just hearing his laugh. He was loud, confident, fast-talking, even faster with his fists. He wore his school blazer like a king wore a cape. When he walked into a room, the air shifted. Even teachers looked at him like he was a fire they couldn't put out.

Alec? He was the quiet one. The one teachers forgot during the roll call. The one whose name they misspelled on certificates. He was smart—smarter than Leon, in fact—but it didn't matter. Brains didn't win crowds. Brains didn't get her attention.

Samantha.

She was the spark that lit the fuse of his hatred. She was kind. Warm. Not too skinny, she had curves in the right place that could rival an angel. She once told Alec his science presentation was "brilliant." For three days, he floated. He believed she saw him.

Until he saw her sneak out of Leon's room one night. Her blouse was inside out. Her hair was a mess. She was laughing.

Alec was in the hallway. Watching. Listening. Dying. He stood there in the dark for hours, hands clenched so hard his nails left moons in his palms. His brother didn't even like Samantha. She was just another name. Another notch. Another disposable soul for Leon to toy with and forget.

That was the moment.

The birth of the rot inside him. The darkness that whispered every night. The anger, the hunger and the need to just kill someone not because he liked it but because he craved for it.

From then on, Alec didn't just want to be seen. He wanted to see Leon fall.

The Years That Followed Alec played the long game. Became the perfect brother. The confidant. Even after he betrayed Leon in Prague the bastard had forgiven him. Leon was stupid, soft and full of himself like Alec didn't deserve his anger.

So, Alec became the perfect brother. The one who smiled and clapped when Leon won again. He learned how to say the right things, nod at the right times, offer advice that subtly led Leon into traps that looked like gifts.

He studied Leon obsessively. Watched his body language. His tone. His schedule. He memorized the way Leon sharpened knives, how he trained with firearms, how he tapped his fingers when annoyed.

He even helped raise Leon's empire from the shadows. Poured in strategies, information, logistics. Leon trusted him. Loved him, even.

And Alec? He counted the days until he could finally take everything.

Then the spider came. Blacky. Leon's prized exotic pet. A rare breed, venomous and beautiful. Alec spent days researching it. He learned how the venom worked; how small doses could imitate a heart attack. How undetectable it was after 48 hours in the bloodstream.

He waited. Planned. Injected the spider's prey with a specific scent that triggered aggression. Left the cage open. Acted surprised. Leon collapsed days later.

Dead. And Alec? He cried. But inside, he was singing. Finally, after years in the shadows. Leon was gone. The world was finally his. And now? He was in Leon's suit, his women, his office.

But it was too much. His Empire.

It was too vast, too tangled. Leon's enemies turned to Alec, smiling with knives behind their backs. Shipments went missing. Loyalty faded. Deals soured. Even the Yakuza smelled blood. The Chinese and Korean wanted nothing from him; they betrayed him just because he was not *LEON the destroyer*.

The power was slipping.

He stood in his office, staring at the LED monitors filled with blinking red alerts—financials, shipments, locations compromised. His hands were trembling.

"This is your fault," he whispered to the screen showing Leon's old portrait.

His own reflection looked back at him.

"You made me small. You made me hate you." Alec hissed, his voice trembling with fury.

He slammed his fists onto the desk. "And now you still haunt me!"

With a deft flick of his wrist, he pulled a chip from his wrist free. His breath hitched as he held it up to the dim light—a quarter-inch nano tracking device, glinting faintly with a malicious sheen.

He flung the tiny device to the ground with a look of pure disgust, his lip curling as though the very sight of it offended him.

Alec stared at it, the blood still running down his arm, and something deep inside him snapped. The device was so small, so insignificant, yet it had been used to control him, to track him like he was nothing more than a piece of property. White-hot rage bubbled up from his core, his vision blurring as anger overtook him.

"You did this to me, Leon" he hissed, his voice trembling with madness. "You bastard... you did this to me. You want to see me all the time huh? You said it was to keep me safe."

Bastard!

But the room went silent. Only his ragged breath echoed. The blood from his wrist dropped to the expensive carpet Leon personally chose.

He could still hear Leon's voice sometimes. That confident, teasing tone. That laugh. It scratched inside Alec's skull like static. It made him furious.

He thought killing him would end it.

But Leon never really died.

Now, Alec was haunted by the ghost of the man he once called "brother"—and it wasn't a ghost that floated in the air. It was a ghost that fought back.

And for the first time, Alec wondered… What if Leon never died? What if the monster he buried was coming back?

His hands twitched. His obsessions deepened. And for a man who once believed himself the mastermind of vengeance—

—he was starting to lose control.

And Catherine? Alec's new obsession?

She smiled at him like a goddess and a devil rolled into one.

Catherine.

That damn woman!

Her voice echoed in his skull like a chime dipped in honey and poison. The memory of her smirk when she stepped out of the casino in that figure-hugging black gown made his pulse spike with something… vile and intimate. A curve of her lips. The sway of her hips. Just like Samantha…his Samantha.

And the smug little nod she gave him.

Like she was taunting him. Like she knew. Like Leon used to.

He watched the surveillance footage again.

Catherine. Mylene. Jhing Jhing.

Three oversized women dressed to kill, strutting into his high-roller floor like queens on a victory march. She didn't flinch. Didn't hesitate. Moved like she built the damn place.

Catherine won a million pounds. One million in two nights.

No normal woman—especially not someone on government support—could do that. But Leon could. Leon knew every trick, every tell, every flaw Alec spent decades hiding in that casino.

And now this woman walked in, flipped the entire board, and left with pockets full of his money and that same goddamn Darrow confidence.

His lips curled. Was it possible?

Was she…?

He slammed his fist through the monitor. Glass shattered like his sanity. Was she Leon's woman?

Few hours later…

"Where the fuck is Mick?"

His guards dragged Mick into the room within minutes.

Mick barely had time to speak before Alec's fist landed in his stomach. The man crumpled to his knees, coughing blood. Alec didn't even pause. He grabbed Mick by the collar and threw him against the wall like a ragdoll.

"I gave you one job. Watch her. Watch Catherine," Alec seethed, pacing like a caged beast. "And what did you do? You let her bleed a million out of my floor like it was Monopoly money!"

Mick wheezed. "She—she just played. I thought she was lucky—"

Alec roared. "Lucky?!"

He kicked Mick so hard in the ribs that something cracked.

"She knew which tables were rigged, which machines weren't. That's Leon's playbook. Not mine. Leon designed that system! So how in God's name did Catherine know it better than me?"

Mick spat blood. "I—I don't know! Maybe she's working with someone—"

Alec yanked a dagger from his desk drawer and drove it into the arm of the chair beside Mick's head. Inches off.

"Wrong answer." He leaned in, his voice a hiss. "You know what I think? I think Catherine isn't who she says she is. I think she's either sleeping with someone from Leon's past—or…"

He swallowed. "Or she is Leon." The thought chilled him.

It thrilled him. It destroyed him. But that's impossible. This was not a fiction novel he was addicted to reading before when he was nothing but a wallpaper. This is real life. This is his life. His…empire.

After his men dragged Mick out—bloodied, broken, but alive—Alec stood alone in his wrecked office. Glass crunched under his shoes. A light flickered above, casting fractured shadows on the blood-stained floor.

He pressed trembling fingers to his lips.

Catherine.

The way she challenged him with her eyes.

The way she turned away, confident he'd follow.

She was dangerous. Clever. Delicious.

She made him feel things. Hatred. Rage. Lust. Fear.

Exactly like Leon used to. He began to crave her. Not just in a man-to-woman way. No. It was more. It was personal. It was an obsession. Alec whispered, half-mad, staring at the blood on his hand.

"If you are Leon's girl...

I will kill you slowly until you beg all the gods." His voice turned dark. "But if you're not—if you're just Catherine—then I'll make you mine. All mine." He walked to the shattered mirror, looked at his own reflection, and whispered with a smirk twisted by madness:

"Either way, Catherine... I'm coming for you."

For five days, Alec Darrow watched her.

Catherine. He'd expected to find the cracks in her mask—secret calls, hidden meetings, cash passed in grocery bags. Anything. Something.

But instead?

She was... boring.

The woman ran errands. Picked up kids from school. Nagged them about unfinished homework. Fell asleep on the couch with a cup of tea she never finished.

She wasn't sleeping with anyone in his circle.

She wasn't wiring funds or meeting black-market dealers.

She was just a plus-sized mom with three noisy children and a penchant for singing off-key while making tuna casserole.

And yet—

She made Alec insane.

He'd wake up thinking of her. Dream of her. The way she smiled at her children. The way she mocked him that night in the casino with her eyes—eyes that shouldn't know his secrets, but did.

Every second that passed, Alec felt himself rot from the inside.

Because Leon was dead.

And Catherine was alive. Too alive. Too familiar. Too good.

So, he called in his best investigator. Told him to dig deeper.

Two days later, Alec stood alone in his dim-lit private viewing room, staring at a paused CCTV frame. The park. A year ago.

Catherine—thinner, paler, younger. Clutching her chest. Collapsing.

And rushing in like a goddamn ghost from the past—

Leon.

Leon Fucking Darrow.

In full clarity. In motion.

Dropping to his knees. Checking her vitals. Tilting her head.

Then—

Mouth-to-mouth. Chest compressions. A call to emergency.

He carried her to his car like she weighed nothing. Drove her to the hospital. Sat beside her for hours. Paid the bills. Signed the discharge form.

What the hell was Leon doing there?

Alec played the footage twenty times.

Thirty.

He knew his brother's face. That arrogant jaw. That cool calculation.

That bastard.

He slammed his fist on the table, shaking the screen.

"This makes no sense!"

His voice echoed in the empty room.

Was she really Leon's girl?

The investigator returned pale-faced.

"I—I traced hospital records. Leon brought her in. Paid in cash. No fake ID. Just said she was a stranger he found."

"And?" Alec barked.

"She had a concussion. Minor brain trauma. She didn't remember anything for three days. But when she woke up…"

The man hesitated.

"She started eating more than she could handle. Like she became a different person. She did nothing but ate."

"Are you sure?"

"Yes, sir."

Alec's breath hitched.

"You're saying Leon met her by accident? That he just happened to be there?"

The man swallowed. "There's no evidence they knew each other before. And after the hospital, there's… nothing. No contact."

Alec's vision blurred.

It couldn't be a coincidence.

Chapter 20

One evening, after yet another chaos in the bathroom and ice cream that tastes like toothpaste and banana.

Finally, I was able to sleep like a baby.

Then the dream...too vivid. Too real. Like a vision from the past, or maybe it was...

It started like a whisper. A breeze.

Children's laughter. The gentle rustling of leaves. A soft blue sky spread wide like a promise above me. I was sitting on a worn wooden bench in the park, arms stretched across the backrest, watching my kids chase each other in zigzags across the grass. I wasn't that huge yet, my face was pale, the dress was too boring.

Jaya's little curls bounced in the sun while I breastfeed her, she was so small, like she just came from me. Very small, cute, her eyes hadn't even opened yet. We were sunbathing for vitamin D.

While Maya's sneakers lit up every time he stomped. Aliya trailed behind, clutching her juice box like it was treasure.

And me? I wasn't... large. Not yet. My body was thinner, lighter, unfamiliar in its frailty. My legs crossed without struggle. My breathing wasn't as heavy. But something felt wrong. I blinked—once. Twice.

The light grew too bright. The air too sharp. My heart? Sluggish. Loud. Wrong. Suddenly, I put the small baby in the picnic blanket.

I gripped my chest. Pain shot like lightning through my left side.

No. No. Not here. Not now.

The world tipped sideways. The grass turned sideways. Screams blurred. My vision shrank into a tunnel of blinding, blinding white.

I collapsed. My face hit the grass. My body spasmed. Everything inside me screamed live, breathe, get up, —but I couldn't move. Not even to call my children's names. My baby….my children. No…No… And then…

Lips. Warm. Firm. Familiar.

On mine.

Breathing air into me like a god. A saviour.

His hands—large, calloused—pressed rhythmically on my chest.

One—two—three—

Again. Again.

Tears stung my eyes. Not from pain. From grief. Please. Not now. Not yet.

Not when my kids were still so small. Not when I was the only one they had. Not when no one else could braid Maya's hair or tuck Aliya in or remind Maya that monsters under the bed were just socks.

My soul—no, something older, something deeper—begged this man, this stranger, to not let me die.

And he didn't.

He breathed for me. Fought for me.

I gasped as breath returned, ragged and painful. I saw his eyes then.

Dark.

Sharp. Unforgiving. Yet... gentle.

He held my hand as I coughed. Cradled my head. Whispered words I couldn't hear but felt deep in my bones.

And then—darkness again.

When I woke up, I was in a sterile white room. IV in my arm. Monitors beeping. I was alive. My babies were safe.

The nurse told me he'd brought me here. Paid for everything. Disappeared before I could say thank you.

Left no name. No number. Only later... only through rumours, whispers, hushed voices in cold hallways... did I learn the truth.

Leon Darrow.

The underworld's ghost. The billionaire. The badass of all badasses. The untouchable kingpin.

The man mothers warned daughters about. And yet—he saved me.

He gave me life again. And in the deepest corners of that dream, I remember wishing... hoping... that if something bad ever happened again, he would be there once more.

Not for me. But for my children.

Because no matter how dark the world could be, I believed that man—my saviour—would guard them like they were his own.

Then...

I woke up with tears on my face. Chest rising too fast. Sweat sticking my shirt to my back.

The apartment was quiet. Kids asleep in their beds. I sat up. Pressed a hand to my chest.

The pain wasn't there anymore—but the memory clung like smoke. This body remembered the pain…the longing, the wish that Leon Darrow saved her children away from darkness. Was it just a dream? I don't think so. It was too vivid. Like it really happened. Or something more?

Because now that I'm Leon—reborn, trapped, alive again—I realized something that chilled me to the marrow.

That day in the park? That wasn't just Catherine's memory.

It was mine. I saved her. I remember now. That woman in the park who collapsed, her children crying in the background. And now I was her. Fate didn't just throw me back into the world. It fused us. It gave me her life. Her children. Her second chance.

And her wish. But it also gave me a mission. Destroy Alec. Protect what's mine. And this time? I won't need saving. I'll be the one who saves. Or the one they fear most.

That after morning after yet another war during breakfast, the wind was gentler this morning. Soft sunlight poured over the familiar benches, warmed the rusted jungle gym, and filtered through the canopy like a golden prayer. Children ran across the grass, their laughter bubbling in the air like champagne fizzing on the surface of something deeper.

I stood at the edge of it all.

Watching.

Clutching the hand of my youngest, Jaya, while Maya chased Aliya toward the sandbox like a maniac on a mission.

We came back here because the kids needed it. They'd been holed up in the apartment too long, and the school week had worn them down.

But me? I needed answers.

The ground beneath my feet—it remembered me. Like it had been waiting. Like every root under the soil whispered, you came back.

I walked slowly, step by step, toward the bench I once collapsed beside. That old wooden thing with its chipped green paint and loose screws. It hadn't changed. But I had.

I sat down, heart heavy and stomach tight. The last time I was here… I died.

No, not Leon.

Catherine. She died for a moment. Her lungs collapsed. Her heart betrayed her. Her panic rose like a tsunami. And it was me—Leon—who saved her. With my hands. With my breath. With that stubborn urge to keep her alive because something inside her—inside us— refused to die.

My fingers brushed the edge of the bench.

Suddenly, it was like I could see it again. The way the sky spun as her head hit the pavement. The way her—my—chest stopped rising. The kids screaming. The way my body knelt beside her, commanding her lungs to obey.

And then—his eyes.

My eyes.

Leon Darrow's eyes looking down at her… at me. It wasn't a dream. Not anymore. I could feel it like a scar pressed into memory. That day, I hadn't just saved a woman—I'd unknowingly saved myself. My future. My second chance.

A pair of joggers passed by, muttering to each other about calories and yoga.

A dog barked in the distance.

Children screamed with joy.

But my heart beat loud in my ears. Thump. Thump. Thump.

Then something odd caught my attention.

A boy with curly hair stumbled near the sandbox. His mom, distracted on her phone, didn't see it.

Before I realized what I was doing, I was already moving.

I reached out, caught him mid-fall just before he cracked his head on the wooden frame. His mom gasped and rushed over with shaky thanks, but I barely registered her words.

Instead, I stared at the boy.

He looked up at me with wide, confused eyes. "Are you an angel?" he asked.

I blinked. "No," I muttered. "Not even close."

Later that day, I sat on the balcony back at the apartment, coffee growing cold in my hand.

Jaya was brushing her doll's hair. Aliya was face-deep in peanut butter crackers and hotdog. Maya snored on the couch with a blanket over her face.

I couldn't shake it.

That park. That bench. That day.

I had saved Catherine, yes.

But what if that was only part of the plan?

What if fate—or karma or whatever the hell was running this circus—had been weaving something deeper?

I didn't just fall into Catherine's body after death. I was tied to her. I'd touched her life before my end. I gave her breath—and now, she was the one giving me life again.

And in this second chance, I had more than revenge to live for.

I had them. The kids. This strange, chaotic, loud little family who looked at me with eyes full of trust and sticky fingers full of joy.

So yeah. I'll return to the park.

I'll return to the underworld. I'll return to hell itself if I have to. Because I wasn't just a mother now. I was Leon Darrow. And I protect what's mine.

Chapter 21

The next day, the rain didn't fall that morning—it hovered. Sky ashy gray, thick with a quiet that made the city feel like it was holding its breath. Not a single leaf stirred. Not even the usual chatter of schoolkids down the hall could break the stillness that slithered through the atmosphere like static.

It was the kind of weather that made you look over your shoulder twice.

And I did. For the third time this week. Because I wasn't paranoid. I was trained.

I knew what surveillance felt like—its heavy stare, the way it clung to the back of your neck like a ghost with a grudge. There was a pattern in the silences between footsteps. A hesitation at corners. A shiver between blinking lights at intersections.

They were here. Alec's men. The bastard was watching me.

I smirked as I pulled my coat tighter and helped Jaya with her scarf. We were going to the small grocery store two blocks down, the one beside the second-hand bookstore and the broken newsstand that sold more gum than newspapers. Aliya and Maya were with the neighbour's kid, distracted by video games and snacks, which gave me time.

Time to confirm what I already knew.

Eyes on me.

At the alley near the end of our building, a car idled.

Black. Tinted windows. The kind of lazy park that meant "we're pretending we belong here."

Please. Amateurs. One of them smoked. Bad habit. Worse for surveillance. I didn't look at them directly, but I made sure the polished edge of my apartment's glass door reflected enough. Man in a cap. Man in a hoodie. No real muscle, but wired the way street dogs are—always hungry, always waiting for a signal.

I felt it deep in my bones. I grinned.

Perfect. This is exactly what I wanted. Let the bastard spiral. Let him lose sleep. Let Alec dig until he rips through the walls of his own sanity.

Later that evening, when the kids had been tucked in, and Aliya clutched her bunny like a lifeline, my burner phone buzzed.

A number I hadn't saved—but I knew the pattern. Joe Smith. My ghost from the past. Hacker. Fixer. The man who knew things no one else should.

I stepped onto the balcony, away from the quiet hum of lullabies and bedtime murmurs.

"Talk," I said.

A crackle on the line. "He found it."

My breath didn't hitch. My fingers didn't even flinch. But my lips curled in a satisfied smirk.

"Found what?"

"The park. CCTV from a year ago—your body—collapsing. Then my friend, Leon—saved her. Mouth to mouth. Hospital records. He's tearing his own files apart trying to stitch the story."

I chuckled under my breath. The game was heating up. I turned my eyes to the misty city below. Rain hadn't fallen yet, but the air was swollen with it. Like everything might snap and pour.

"He'll dig deeper," Joe warned. "He's... not sleeping. Rumour is he's obsessed. Losing it."

"Good," I whispered. "Let him."

Let Alec unravel the way I once did. Let him fall for the mystery he created. Because what hurts more than a brother you betrayed?

A woman you can't have. And I had become both.

It was a week later when he returned the car.

Alec. Cleaned, polished. Repaired like new. Parked right at the curb outside our building like some gallant knight dragging a defeated dragon back to its queen.

I knew the minute he stepped out of that matte black sedan of his. Hair too neat. Cufflinks sharp. Tie twisted just right to look effortless. A calculated effort to look casual.

The weather was colder then, the wind sharper. I was in jeans and a hoodie, hair tied up. Kids yelling behind me about who spilled milk on whose homework.

He handed over the keys with a smile too slow, too soft. "Thought you might need her back." Alec's expression didn't change; his lips still set in that hard line.

I stared at the SUV. I missed her, sure. But I didn't like what the gesture meant.

He lingered.

I acted like a damsel again.

Thanks Netflix Christmas cringey drama.

I looked up at him, feeling the hot sting of tears pricking the corners of my eyes, but I refused to let them fall. I need to show how happy I was, like I owed him so much that my life was not even enough to pay his chivalry.

I acted good.

My anger was my armour.

My pain was my weapon.

Finally, he spoke, his voice low, calm, but carrying an edge of danger. "That coffee you promised," he said. "Maybe now?" His eyes flicked up to meet mine, sharp and serious.

I tilted my head, giving him the kind of smile that said not today, sugar. "Sorry. Diapers, school, and disaster. Maybe next time. Thanks anyway. I owe you one."

There was no next time.

There was no next time.

And he knew it.

I shut the door before he could ask again.

Because I knew men like him.

The obsessed ones. The clever ones. The ones who thought the world bent at their desire.

And I was no longer the woman who bent. *I am Leon, the drama-queen-from-Netflix.*

That night, I sat now in the living room, kids asleep, with a glass of wine in one hand and tomorrow's grocery list in the other.

But I wasn't thinking of eggs or bread.

I was thinking of Alec.

Of his obsession brewing like a storm. He wanted answers. I was the answer.

Leon Darrow in flesh.

In womanhood. In disguise.

But he didn't know that.

For him, I'm just Leon's girl.

Let him come. Let him watch. Let him burn with the madness of questions he couldn't solve.

Because soon, I'd give him a new obsession.

Desire.

And when he begged to understand who I really was, I'd make him choke on every drop of regret he tried to swallow.

The moment I saw the man again—the one who had been watching me from across the street for days—I felt a sick lurch in my stomach. He was standing too close to the playground gate. My children were inside, laughing and running, completely unaware of the way his eyes lingered, always a beat too long. I had warned him once already. But today, something in me snapped.

I pushed my stroller with force, my heart hammering in my chest. I could hear Jhing Jhing calling out behind me, but the ringing in my ears drowned out everything else. My babies—my heart—were in that playground. And this man had crossed a line.

He didn't flinch when I approached, but he underestimated me.

"Who sent you?!" I demanded, grabbing his collar. His eyes widened.

"I don't know what you're talking ab—"

I punched him. Hard. The pain in my knuckles was nothing compared to the fire in my veins. He stumbled backward, landing with a grunt.

My children, startled by the noise, began to cry.

Their terrified wails cut through the chaos like knives.

I saw Jhing Jhing running toward them, trying to scoop them into her arms, but the scene was spiralling.

The man tried to stand, but I was already calling the police.

By the time they arrived, I had restrained him with help from a few passersby—bless them—and my hands were trembling.

Not from fear anymore.

From rage. From helplessness. From the betrayal that had been festering inside me since I began suspecting Alec was behind it all.

Of course it was Alec again.

They took him in, cuffed and defiant.

But the surveillance camera—the one facing the playground gate—had mysteriously been broken. Smashed, as if someone knew it would be the only visual proof.

That night, my home was too quiet despite the kids already asleep. I sat in the dark with a cup of green tea gone cold, trying to make sense of everything.

Then the call came.

He died.

Three hours after being placed in the holding cell, the man was found dead.

No signs of external trauma. Just dead.

I knew, deep in my gut, who had made the call to the police in the first place. Alec.

He wanted to show me that he was watching over me, that this was all part of his design. I almost laughed at the irony.

He was watching from behind the scenes. Puppeteering everything.

So I played my part.

The scared woman.

I called him. I pretended I needed comfort.

That I didn't know what was going on.

That I was frightened. I even let my voice tremble.

And like a shadow breaking free from the darkness, he came.

He didn't call. He didn't message. He just appeared at my door.

Got you asshole.

"I came as soon as I heard," Alec said, stepping into my foyer like he still had a right to be there. His shirt was wrinkled—deliberately so, I guessed—and his eyes were filled with an emotion I couldn't quite name.

Concern? Possession?

Or guilt. *Impossible.*

I clutched a throw blanket around my shoulders, standing just far enough to make it look like I still trusted him.

He looked around as if expecting to find bloodstains on the walls. "Are the kids, okay?"

I nodded; my voice small. "They're asleep." I blinked, my act faltering because, right now, in my apartment, in Catherine's apartment, *I want to kill him.*

But no...not now. The game was far from over.

"Catherine..." He stepped closer, his voice lowering. "I don't think it's safe for you to be here alone. I can call someone to stay with you, or—"

I stepped back. "No. I just needed to see a familiar face. Someone to talk to."

His expression softened. I could see him drop his guard, just a little.

Good. I would let him think he still had control—for now.

Then we talk for hours, talking about anything under the sun.

Then he left with a smirk of a man that was sure of himself.

Too sure that he had me under his palm.

In your dreams dickhead.

Chapter 22

The Police Station - Next Morning

I walked into the precinct holding Jhing Jhing's hand, while Mylene followed behind with the kids. The station was a sea of chaos. Reporters loitered outside. The air inside was dry, cold, and smelled of sweat and stress.

The officer at the front desk barely looked up.

"We're here about the man who died in custody," I said.

Before the officer could respond, Jhing Jhing lost it.

"Your damn people let that man die!" she shouted, slamming her palm on the counter. "He was the only one who could tell us what's going on! And now you expect us to sit back while you file paperwork?!"

The officers turned. One stood. The tension grew thick.

Mylene tried to calm her down, but she was already in tears too. "We're mothers! What if the next guy goes after our kids? What if—what if Catherine hadn't stopped him?! You didn't even protect the one lead we had!"

I clutched my coat tighter around me, tears welling in my eyes—but not just from grief. From exhaustion.

From fear. Of course, I need to act like I'm about to lose it.

"I want the surveillance camera footage pulled," I said, my voice low and steady.

"It was broken," an officer said. "Before the incident."

Convenient.

Too convenient.

I bit down on my lip until I tasted blood. This was really how Alec played.

Behind me, Mylene was now sobbing into a tissue. "We've all been followed. Watched. We thought it was nothing. But now someone's dead, and we're being told nothing?"

One of the detectives finally motioned for us to follow him.

"We'll take your statements," he said, guiding us into a cramped, too-bright room.

And I thought, as I sat down under the flickering fluorescent light—

Alec made sure the man couldn't talk. He knew I was getting too close. So he took care of it. Silently. Efficiently. Coldly. But he made one mistake.

He thought I'd be scared enough to run back to him.

He didn't realize I was done playing the victim.

I am *Leon fuckng Darrow*. I was the shadow crawling behind the thrones of kings and the silence before the trigger is pulled. I didn't answer to the gods—I made devils kneel.

And I ate half eaten apple jam and sardine sandwich from five days ago as a snack.

The coffee shop was not ready for us. The bell above the door chimed politely as we entered—but what followed was anything but polite.

Seven children.

Two strollers. One toddler escape artist. Three sugar-starved pre-teens. A diaper bag that looked like a refugee emergency kit. And one four-year-old asking loudly, "Does this place have chicken nuggets??"

They did not.

We descended like a hurricane.

Mylene had her twin girls, armed with pink toy cars and a pathological need to throw them into innocent civilians' ankles. Jhing Jhing carried her baby strapped to her chest like a tiny war general, while her daughter ran ahead screaming "CUPCAKES!" as if she was declaring war.

Me? I had Jaya wiping chocolate milk off his face using the dog's hoodie he passed on the sidewalk, Maya trying to order ten brownies in a British accent, and Aliya pretending to faint dramatically because *"I haven't had sugar in six hours."*

I gave the barista a one-hundred-pound tip before the situation escalated into a lawsuit.

"Hi, I'm sorry in advance," I said sweetly. "Please bring us every sweet you have. If it has sugar, we'll take it. Keep the change. Also... do you offer therapy in the back?"

The poor guy just blinked, nodded, and waved us to a corner table as if guiding a herd of goats.

We crammed ourselves into a long booth. The kids took over one half with a mountain of brownies, croissants, and frappes that could induce cardiac arrest.

Chocolate smeared everything: cheeks, noses, table, probably someone's shoe.

I sipped my overpriced pink latte and leaned in. "So..." I said in a hush-hush tone, "a guy died in police custody last night huh."

"Yes, I call this too cliche?" Jhing Jhing gasped, mid-bite into a blueberry muffin. "Sounds murder to me?"

"Agree," I said. "Convulsed. Bleeding. Foamed at the mouth. Textbook overkill."

Mylene cringed. "Shit. I can't help but want to rewatch *Dexter* again on Netflix."

"Yep. The asshole deserves it and the same creep who stalked me in the park a few days ago. The one who pretended to ask for directions and kept looking at my chest like it had answers."

"Men are pigs," Jhing Jhing said, as Ivy dropped an entire cookie into her Frappuccino. She didn't blink. Just drank it anyway.

I leaned back and watched as Aliya licked chocolate from the window like a bored cat. "His death? Too convenient. It stinks of Alec."

Mylene snorted into her mocha. "Isn't everything Alec's fault these days?"

"Yes," I said with a straight face. "Even this overpriced strawberry pink croissant. Probably Alec's fault."

"You think he killed the stalker?" Jhing Jhing asked, pulling a sticker out of her baby's hair. "To protect you or…?"

I raised my eyebrow. "To cover his tracks. Or to scare me. Or maybe to impress me. You know how psychopaths are—dead bodies are their love language."

"Ahhh so romantic," Mylene muttered, feeding her toddler a spoon of whipped cream while he screamed for a cinnamon roll "that looks like a snail!"

"Ladies, focus." I dropped my voice lower. "He's watching me. He has people on the street. He returned my SUV, he's offering coffee like he's courting me, and now someone dies in police custody who just happened to stalk me?"

Drama…

I couldn't help but smile inside, my girls, my friends were really something else, it felt like I truly belonged to this mayhem though I already had a plan but still, I just couldn't help myself and asked for their opinion, mom-sass-jean opinion was always better.

Jhing Jhing nodded slowly. "He's spiraling."

"Spiraling into a Catherine-shaped abyss," Mylene added.

I smirked. "Exactly. I want him to be obsessed. I want him to be confused that he wouldn't even recognize a blueberry muffin from a wet-dirty diaper.

Mylene smirked, "Exactly, we can't let him know we were pulling the strings."

I smirked like a badass rotten Dorito, "I need ideas. What do we do next—subtly?"

Jhing choked on her latte. "Subtle? Catherine, you faked fainting in front of your ex back in college just to get free croissants."

"That was strategy," I corrected.

"You hacked a slot machine using a black lipstick USB drive."

"Efficiency."

"You told the barista your name was Muffin Blueberry just so Alec's men couldn't track your drink orders."

Mylene cackled. "Okay that one was sexy, I'll give you that."

As we tried to plot, the kids hit stage-four sugar combustion.

One of the twins tried to eat a straw wrapper. Maya stacked six brownies into a sandwich. Aliya was giving another child a motivational speech about chocolate addiction. Jaya and Ivy staged a dramatic faint again—on the pastry display.

Jhing Jhing threw a napkin over her face. "We're going to get banned."

Mylene, juggling her baby and her dignity, leaned in. "Listen. If you want Alec to stay obsessed but confused, we need a two-pronged attack."

I raised an eyebrow. "Go on."

"One—continue being too perfect. Bake cookies, volunteer at school, look like a Pinterest board threw up on your house. But occasionally—slip. Say something only the devil would say."

I grinned. "Like threatening the neighbour with a rusty spoon?"

"Exactly."

Mylene leaned in closer as if she was telling me the formula of Coca-Cola, "We all knew that his brother died right? The fucking Leon Darrow? I heard it was Alec who killed the poor guy, rest his soul."

Eh?

I almost spit my overpriced latte.

Me? Poor guy?

Me, the Assassin of Sass?

The Kingpin of Diapers and Tea Cups?

Chapter 23

Jhing Jhing added, "Ha! I have an idea…or two—"

"What is it?" I swore I could read her bearing inside juggling like a tornado of rotten milk of badness.

Then she leaned in closer to my ear, "Leave a trail. Just a tiny breadcrumb. Something from Leon's life. A book only Leon loved. A cigar stub in his purse. Something small. Let him question everything. Make him crazy."

Note to self: Do not, I repeat, do not mess with this woman. She is a Filipina warrior incarnate.

Mylene rolled her eyes, "And how do you suggest we do that? We don't even know that Leon guy."

Ha! "Easy…We have the internet, silly." Jhing Jhing grumbled with the same confidence of Mr. Trump when he said, *'I will make America proud again.'* Proud my ass.

"Ohhh, I like it." Mylene tapped her well-manicured fingers. "Let him unravel on his own. Make him dig."

"Make him paranoid?" I said with glee. "Make him think Leon never died."

…cliche

We sat there, sipping lattes like witches in mom jeans, plotting emotional destruction while seven kids smeared frosting on each other's foreheads.

And I? I laughed. Because chaos was mine.

Alec thought he was playing chess. He didn't know I was writing the damn rulebook using a little pony pen that was bitten by chaos and regrets.

*****

Alec's Office — Early Evening

The room was dim, sterile, and tense—like a funeral parlor with a dress code. The heavy scent of cologne fought with the bitter smell of coffee and expensive stress.

Alec sat behind his desk, sleeves rolled up, tie askew, staring down a new report like it had personally insulted his ancestors.

"Sir," Mick said, clearing his throat. "We had another visual on Catherine today."

Alec's eyes flicked up. "Where?"

Mick groaned, "She drop-off at her kid's school. She yelled at a crossing guard."

"Normal," Alec said dryly.

"Then she gave another mom a protein bar from the Russian black market."

"…Also, still normal."

"And then—" Mick hesitated.

Alec arched a brow. "Spit it out."

"She… lit a cigar."

What the…

Silence. Utter silence. Not a pin could drop—it would've shattered the tension like a bomb.

Alec stood. Slowly. Eyes narrowed. "She what?"

"Lit a cigar, sir."

Alec's hands curled into fists. "What kind of cigar."

Mick pulled out a blurry photo. "Vintage Arturo Fuente, limited run, Havana-scented wrap. Leon's favourite."

Alec stared at the image. A grainy snapshot of Catherine—her curls tied in a messy bun, oversized sunglasses sliding down her nose, one hip cocked as she waved goodbye to a school bus—with a burning cigar between two dainty fingers like she was James Bond's personal chef. "Jesus," Alec whispered.

She even had the damn angle right.

He sank into his chair.   It hit him—like a brick of déjà vu. Leon. Standing outside their private high school dorm, leaning on a wall like he was the cover of a mafia-themed teen magazine. Cigar between two fingers. Charcoal suit. Girls flocking like pigeons to breadcrumbs.

Alec had once tried to smoke that same cigar, just to look cool. He nearly died coughing while Leon laughed for five straight minutes and patted his back like a benevolent jackass. And now? That exact brand. That exact lean. On Catherine.

His brain short-circuited.

What the f*ck is happening?

*****

Meanwhile, in a messy apartment lit by weak sunlight, Catherine (a.k.a. Leon in mom mode) was wiping frosting off Aliya's shirt with one hand and mixing boxed red brownies with the other.

I absolutely meant to light that cigar in front of the school pickup line. It was an art., Ha! I did it slowly, dramatically, between yelling at Jaya to stop licking the gate and Maya to stop asking random parents if they had Wi-Fi and free pink donuts.

I'd felt the watcher across the street. Alec's man. Always in sunglasses. Always pretending to fix a bike that didn't exist.

I made eye contact, took a long drag of the cigar, and winked.

Not flirtatiously. Menacingly. Then coughed once, because let's be honest—it'd been a while.

*****

Back in Alec's office, he had the footage playing on loop. His jaw clenched tighter with each playback.

"Why the hell would she smoke that cigar?"

"She said, and I quote," Mick added helpfully, *"'A gift from a dead man. Strong as hell, but sweet and spicy at the end.'* Then she patted a pink-lunchbox shaped like a dinosaur and left."

Alec's eye twitched. That was a Leon line.

Fuck! Word for word. He used to say it at poker tables. At parties. After executions.

Alec's heart pounded in his chest like a war drum. Catherine had no access to Leon's past. No connection. Except…That damn park footage. That one random act of CPR. Leon saved her once. Could it be?

No. It's not possible. *Is it?*

Later that night, Alec sat alone in his penthouse office. Rain tapped on the tall windows like tiny fingers. He stared at a single file: Catherine's profile. Beside it, Leon's—now marked deceased.

Same birthdate? No. Same style? Unlikely. Same presence?

His fingers trembled.

Then his phone buzzed. A picture. Blurry. The side of Catherine's face today at the café.

She was laughing. Wildly. With Jhing Jhing. With Mylene. The three of them chaotic and vibrant, surrounded by kids eating brownies like they were going extinct.

But her laugh… It was his. It was like Leon.

Alec shut the screen off and pressed his palm to his face.

"I buried you," he whispered.

And yet here you are.

In lipstick and green leopard-print leggings.

A ghost with a baby sippy cup and a vengeance.

Impossible…

Chapter 24

The next day, of course, I texted the girls that it was time to send some drama.

Me: *Emergency brunch. Expensive coffee. Bring chaos. No kids. Except Jaya, because she's basically my tiny wallet inspector.*

I got there first with Jaya, who was busy interrogating a croissant like it owed her lunch money. She had one shoe off, blue juice spilled on her yellow green new dress, and was currently feeding a sugar packet to a plush rabbit.

Location: *Café Très Pretensieux*

Okay I know I just made it up, but yes, I'm acting like the real Catherine now as I looked at the place with regal mama eyes. *(A place that charged £11 for toast and had a chandelier in the bathroom)*

Perfect chaos energy. Mylene arrived next—fresh-faced, hair blown out, zero under-eye bags like she slept on clouds woven by angels. "The nanny," she said, sipping an oat milk matcha like it cured diseases, "is a gift from the gods. I even shaved both legs this morning."

"Show-off," I muttered, digging for a wet wipe.

Then came Jhing Jhing, Ivy in tow, pushing a stroller with one hand and a portable smart fridge manual in the other. She looked like she hadn't slept since 2003. "Ivy hacked my fridge," she announced dramatically. "Now it tells me what kind of mood I'm in based on how many times I open the door."

Mylene blinked. "You okay?"

"No. The *knock knock fridge* said I'm emotionally unstable and suggested soup. The *washing machine* agrees."

We ordered overpriced green lattes of Koreans, one babyccino, and a £9 muffin we all stared at in silence because it looked too pretty to eat and yet not good enough to justify its rent. I leaned in, swirling my coffee. "Okay. I may have lit Leon's cigar at the school drop-off line yesterday."

Mylene froze mid-sip. "You didn't."

Jhing Jhing gasped. "*The Arturo Fuente?!*"

"Yep."

Even Jaya blinked at me. Ivy sneezed like it was timed. I leaned back. "Alec's men were watching. I made sure. I even did the lean."

Mylene shrieked into her coffee cup. "OH MY GOD YOU DID THE LEON LEAN? The one with the hip pop?"

"With the lip twitching." I smirked.

"Bitch. You are bold."

"Terrifying," Jhing Jhing muttered, eyes wide with reverence. "Alec's probably chewing drywall."

"Good." I grinned and broke a muffin in half like it was a declaration of war.

"I want him *obsessed*," I said. "I want him to see me and think, '*is it Catherine or the brother I want to murder after high school biology class?*'"

Mylene raised her hand. "We need more breadcrumbs."

"More ghost echoes," Jhing Jhing agreed.

"Okay, okay," Mylene tapped her phone. "How about this. You show up somewhere only Leon would go. Like—"

"His private cigar lounge?" Jhing Jhing supplied. "Ooh. With a whiskey bottle signed by Leon's ex-accountant."

We cackled. "OR," Mylene said, slapping the table, "borrow his old cologne. *The Guerlain Homme one.*"

"Jesus," I said. "That smell would haunt a man."

Jhing Jhing leaned in. "Do you have any old recordings of Leon?"

"Yes, I asked the cousin of a friend that knows a friend who has a friend that knows about Leon…"

Of course, I am THE recording.

"Lovely." They shrieked again.

"Also," I added sweetly, "I changed my ringtone to *'Dancing Queen.'* The one Leon used to play on repeat before he sent people to the afterlife." The table fell silent in reverent chaos.

"Girl." Mylene whispered. "How the hell did you get such intel? Are you sure you're not selling your soul to the devil?"

"You're unhinged." Jhing Jhing clutched her latte.

I grinned. "Of course not." *I am the devil.... with pink sass.*

The waiter came to drop off the bill, visibly afraid of the sheer estrogen-based anarchy at the table.

"Tip's already paid," I smiled, slipping him a hundred-pound note and a wink.

"Sorry about the kids' crumbs," Mylene added as Jaya kicked sugar packets across the floor. The man nodded like he'd survived a war. We left in chaotic silence—heels clicking, strollers wobbling, muffin crumbs trailing us like a warning sign.

Then. We laughed, loud and unfiltered. The kind of laughter that rolls from your ribs when you know someone else is suffering far away, probably curling into a silk-lined corner of their expensive shame. But even as I laughed, even as I sipped the perfect pink water bottle of war, I could feel it crawling just beneath my skin. A hollow rage. Deep. Personal. I hated Alec. I hated that I was breathing the same air as him. That after everything he had taken, everything he had destroyed, he still dared to exist. He should've been dust by now.

Forgotten. Like a bad name in a worse dream. But no. He was still here. And somewhere, not far from this overpriced café, *Alec Darrow* was probably screaming into a pillow stuffed with guilt, vintage goose feathers, and Chanel No. 5. Just as I intended.

And it was only *Thursday*.

The next day, it was the kind of gloomy afternoon that felt like the world needed a nap. Thick grey clouds hung over the sky like soggy cotton balls, and the breeze tasted faintly of impending drama and someone's burnt lasagna from the apartment above.

The *Kore@n Café* was stupidly luxurious. Outdoor seating lined with silk-cushioned chairs, each table adorned with minimalist glass vases holding flowers that screamed, *"We don't grow in this climate, we're imported."* A violinist in the corner played a sad indie version of "Toxic" by Britney Spears. A couple of influencers nearby were pretending to drink coffee for pictures they'd later caption *"morning peace."*

And then *we* arrived.

Us: *A parade of chaos in Target mom fits and murder-level makeup.*

Me, Jhing-Jhing, and Mylene marched in like we owned the world—or were about to destroy it with glitter and unresolved trauma. Jaya skipped beside me in a violet sort tutu, Ivy clutched a bag of rainbow marshmallows like it was her emotional support pet, and the girls? They were ready.

The cafe hummed with espresso machines, clinking porcelain, and the sounds of people pretending to work on their novels. A barista with a nose ring shaped like a lightning bolt was aggressively frothing milk like it had wronged his ancestors. Someone was arguing on a podcast in the corner. I was seated in the middle of this latte-scented storm, sipping bitterness and plotting like the momma warlord I had become.

Alec was already seated at a far table, pretending not to be watching.

Too bad his eyes never left us.

Earlier, I called Joe Smith and asked if he found something new. And yes, he told me that Alec Fucking Darrow was here, fake drinking a huge white Frappuccino espresso.

We ordered and sat at the next empty table like we owned the place. I held my usual overpriced latte like it was a wine glass. Dainty. Elegant. A proper British woman who definitely didn't used to smuggle venom in heel compartments and blow-up docks before brunch.

I could feel his stare. Like knives. Or worse—like feelings. I refused to meet his gaze, instead focused on buttering a scone with an energy that screamed "unbothered queen."

Mylene slid into the seat beside me, whispering, *"He's twitching."*

Jhing-Jhing took off her trench coat to reveal a red turtleneck that screamed "conspirator," then added, *"His jaw clenched when you licked the butter knife."*

"I was hungry," I said, taking a delicate bite. "Also… that's the same twitch Leon used to have when he planned someone's slow, painful downfall."

"Mm. Karma's buttery," Mylene muttered, slapping jam on toast like it owed her child support.

Chapter 25

Meanwhile, *Alec* sat across the terrace at a black marble table, nursing the Frappuccino espresso like it might help him make sense of the nightmare fever dream that was Catherine.

He had files. Photos. Surveillance. Documents that should have made her just a regular woman with mom issues and a mild *Pinterest & Amazon* addiction. But no. She was unpredictable. Terrifying. Familiar in ways that haunted him at 3AM.

And now she was wearing Leon's exact scent. *Guerlain Homme.*

Why the f*ck would she wear that? He crushed a sugar cube in his fist and called Mick under his breath. "Find out what perfume she uses."

Mick: *"It's not listed in her file, sir. But... her café order is identical to Leon's."*

Alec stared across the terrace.

Catherine tilted her head, ran a finger over her lower lip, then laughed—Leon's laugh. That smug, slow, almost-purring chuckle that used to haunt Alec through high school corridors.

His hands were trembling.

"Sir?" Mick asked. "Are you okay?"

"I'm fine," Alec hissed, even as his espresso cup cracked in his grip.

He lingered in the shadows, watching, waiting, his mind ablaze with plans and curses. Soon, he promised himself. Soon, he would cast aside the chains Catherine had placed on him. Soon, he would rise as the ruler he was meant to be, and all those who had dared to oppose him would be forced to kneel or be crushed underfoot.

Mylene sipped her oat milk chai like she wasn't helping orchestrate psychological warfare. "Okay. Let's recap what we've done."

Jhing Jhing ticked items off on her iPad like a soccer coach from hell.

"Stage one: Leon lean at school pick-up."

"Stage two: Cigars at the gas station."

"Stage three: Scent warfare."

"Stage four: Random Latin phrases whispered near his men."

We brainstorm like our lives depended on it while the *café* was the kind of place where the air itself felt overpriced. Everything smelled like roasted ambition and lavender sanitizer. Light jazz oozed from invisible speakers, barely audible over the gentle clack of a thousand *MacBooks*. Patrons lounged like caffeinated royalty—graphic designers in beanies pretending to work on indie games, law students with five empty espresso shots lined up like trophies, and influencer moms staging a photo shoot with their baby's half-eaten croissant. One woman was definitely in a Zoom meeting with a judge.

Another man next to the fake plant was probably writing a manifesto. It was the kind of joint where people judged you not by your drink, but by your laptop sticker aesthetic and your ability to pronounce *"cortado"* without blinking.

"Today is *Stage Five*," I said, raising my cup like a toast to war. The plan was in motion, the trap set. While I was basking in my internal villain monologue, Jaya tugged on my shirt and, with wide hopeful eyes, asked if she could breastfeed again—for comfort, she claimed. I declined with grace and maternal exhaustion, handing her an overpriced cookie the size of a full moon instead. It was so large, *NASA* probably charged royalties.

Naturally, she screamed two seconds later after spilling cocoa on her glittery left shoe like her life was over. Not to be outdone, Ivy—sweet chaos incarnate—somehow managed to drop not one, not two, but three fluffy marshmallows into the open tote bag of the woman behind us. The woman didn't even flinch. She didn't even look. This was the kind of café where if a child set fire to a croissant, someone would just raise their eyebrow and say, *"How postmodern."*

That's when I felt it.

That shift in the air.

The way static prickled my skin. Like I was being watched by a very specific ghost.

Across the way, he stood.

Alec. My dear brother. The man who once wore my trust like a suit and then poisoned me with my own bloody spider.

His face was calm. Too calm. Calm like a lake before it drowns you.

I could practically smell his rage. The confusion. The rising tide of obsession rolling off him like cologne he stole from someone richer. He adjusted his coat slowly—too slowly—like a man preparing to commit arson but wanted to look good doing it.

Then, he walked over. Smooth. Controlled.

Like a shark who discovered hot yoga and had something to prove.

I braced.

Mylene lifted her coffee to her lips like it was a sniper rifle.

Jhing-Jhing casually slid her glitter lip gloss across the table like a rogue offering me a dagger made of *glitter and pettiness*.

He arrived, his shadow darkening our table like a cursed weather forecast.

"Catherine," he said, voice smoother than the caramel drizzle on Ivy's stolen cookie.

I looked up and blinked, all honey and saccharine sweetness.

"Alec. Didn't see you there." Lies. I saw you the second your expensive shoes crossed the tile like you owned the ground.

"Of course not," he said coolly. "You've been… busy."

Good. He noticed. You should. I've been driving you insane with a sugar-sweet vengeance.

"Croissants can be demanding," I replied, biting into mine like it owed me rent.

He stared. Hard. Digging. Searching for cracks. Weakness. The ghost of Leon smirking behind my eyes dared him to find even a whisper.

But there was nothing.

I was Catherine. I am Catherine. The rainbow cupcake mom. Alec waking nightmare in yoga pants. The wild-card soon-to-be widow, because I swore, one more call from Stupid-Ray I might lose it.

And then—

"Mommy, are you going to light another cigar at school tomorrow?" Jaya asked in a voice that carried across three tables and probably into Alec's soul.

BOOM. He flinched. Like I slapped him with my old assassin resume. Alec blinked. Once. Twice. His soul left his body and probably ran down the street screaming.

I calmly handed Jaya another moon-cookie. "Shhh, baby. That was our secret."

Alec exhaled like he'd just been shot with a memory. "You're… different," he said, his voice husky with denial.

"Motherhood changes people, Alex," I said, sipping my latte like it was blood from my enemies.

"Not this much." His eyes begged to sit beside me, to pry, to seduce, to control.

But Jhing-Jhing moved first, sliding her oversized Brown Prada bag onto the empty seat like a barricade made of tax returns and sharp elbows. Her smile said *'back off or I'll rearrange your spine with my high heels.'*

"Or maybe," I said, meeting his cold gaze with something ancient and sharp, "you just never really knew me."

He said nothing. He just stood there. Haunted. Hollowed out.

Absolutely feral inside.

The ghost of Leon grinned inside my chest.

And as Alec turned to walk away, retreating step by step like a general realizing his army was made of whipped cream and poor decisions, I smirked.

'Phase Five' almost complete.

Also, I really needed a refill. But first, revenge.

"He totally pooped his Armani boxers," Mylene said, not even bothering to whisper. Her lips curled in smug satisfaction, one leg crossed over the other, her huge Gucci sunglasses reflecting the afternoon sun like some mafia heiress ready to order a hit with her next sip of oat milk latte.

"He's going to burn all his photos of Leon tonight," Jhing-Jhing added between bites of almond tart, then—without pause—launched into an elaborate tale about how her new *washing machine* had a built-in voice assistant that told her she should consider having one more child to optimize laundry cycles. "She said it with concern, okay? Like a disappointed auntie! What kind of AI makes fertility suggestions?!"

I snorted into my coffee, but it came out more like a growl. My hand tightened around the croissant like it had personally offended me. I bit into it hard, feeling the golden flakes explode onto the tabletop like edible confetti.

"Good." The butter was perfect. The pastry warm and crisp. And the coffee? Bitter. Sharp. Darker than the thoughts I had about Alec. Just like my brother's heart—if he had one left at all.

The clouds above finally broke, sunlight slanting through the café's crystal awning, casting golden bars over the marble table and glass teacups like divine prison stripes. The world lit up like it was proud of me. Proud of the ghost I had become. Proud of the game I was playing. I imagined the sun high-fiving a thundercloud while whispering, "Get him, girl."

"Let's start *Phase Six*," I said, my voice light, sugar-laced, but inside I was thrumming with something darker.

Rage. Vindication.

The taste of unfinished war on the back of my tongue.

"Which is?" Mylene asked, her diamond-crusted manicure tapping the table. Her hair—too glossy, too expensive, too victorious—bounced as she turned toward me. Everything about her screamed, *I beat your casino, now I'm just playing for fun.*

I grinned. It was slow. Hungry.

Like a lion who smelled blood on the wind.

I wanted Alec unhinged. *Confused*. I wanted to slip into the edges of his mind and make him question every memory, every moment. I wanted him pacing his glass-walled office, whispering "Leon?" into the dark like a man haunted by a ghost he helped bury.

"Send him a bouquet," I said, sliding my phone toward Jhing-Jhing who already had three florists saved under 'Doom Petals.'

"Include Leon's old signature card." My voice lowered as I quoted it.

"To the brother who tried but failed. – L.D."

Jaya cheered with her chocolate-smeared fingers high in the air like she just won a pageant. Ivy let out a heroic burp that echoed off the glass and made the influencer couple next to us grimace.

Outside, the weather had turned beautifully sinister. Sunshine pierced through gaps in the clouds like divine lasers aimed directly at Alec's carefully constructed ego. A light breeze swirled the smell of freshly baked pastries, burned hopes, and the very real scent of caramelized pride. It was the perfect day for psychological warfare with a side of almond milk.

Chapter 26

*T*he moment *Alec disappeared around the corner*—his trench coat flapping like it was mad too—the café exhaled with me.

"Well, damn," Mylene muttered, fanning herself with a café loyalty card she'd never use. "That man looked like he just saw your ghost… and married it… and the ghost took the house."

I was still grinning, my croissant flaking triumphantly all over my overpriced leggings. *"And again, Phase Five was now a success."*

"He looked pale," Jhing-Jhing added.

"Like he just realized he was the side character in your revenge novel."

"Mommy," Jaya whispered, peering out the window, "is that man coming back with a bazooka?"

I blinked. "No, baby. That's just how the poor man walks."

Ivy, now using her marshmallows as poker chips to bribe the barista for extra whipped cream, snorted. "He looked like a farted secret."

The table exploded in laughter.

Even the quiet barista, who'd been eavesdropping since *Phase Two*, chuckled behind the espresso machine.

The chaos resumed in waves.

Jaya tried to steal my lipstick. Ivy tried to climb the plant stand. Mylene was on her fourth coffee, eyes wide, heart rate matching the stock market.

Jhing-Jhing somehow Face Timed her robot fridge to ask it how many eggs she had left. *The fridge* responded in a calm robotic tone: *"Please stop buying organic air. You are over budget."*

We laugh so hard. It was refreshing. It was a good laugh.

Meanwhile, a man at the next table was furiously typing a screenplay titled "Love and Lattes: A Barista's Reckoning" and paused only to look up at our table with the kind of wariness reserved for hurricanes and unpredictable divorcees.

I leaned in.

"Phase Six. It's time."

I grinned, reaching into my bag like a magician revealing the next trick. "The rose and the card."

Mylene snapped her fingers. "Spray it with that cologne Leon used to wear! The one that smelled like sin and broken men!"

"Already done," I said, sipping dark roast like it was vengeance.

Jaya, still sticky with cookies, saluted me like a tiny general.

Outside, the wind picked up.

Somewhere, Alec probably opened a window, saw the rose on his desk, and had to take his third anxiety pill of the morning. He would never admit it—but the scent, the handwriting, the vibe—it would eat at him.

He would stay up all night reviewing handwriting samples. He would call Mick or his ex-wife *whatever*.

He would interrogate florists. He would Google *"can ghosts forge letters?"* at 3 a.m. in his silent penthouse while staring at Leon's last photo.

He would lose sleep. And maybe some hair.

And we?

We will be back here tomorrow, same café, same seat, same sugar-sticky kids—plotting the next phase.

ALEC's Office – The next morning

The scent of the rose still lingered.

It sat on his desk like a cursed relic, its soft crimson petals mocking him. A single drop of water glistened at the edge like a tear he'd never admit to shedding. The handwriting was flawless. Too flawless. He had flipped it over seventeen times. Held it to the light. Pressed his thumb to it to feel the texture of the ink.

"It's him. It's Leon," he whispered like a confession to the dead. Leon had moulded him into this creature of resentment, pushing him to the edge, blaming him, denying him the validation he had once craved as a child. Alec's heart ached with the injustices he had suffered, yet in his twisted mind, he found it easier to play the victim than to confront the depths of his anger.

He clenched the note in his fist, crushed it with all the restraint of a man teetering on the edge of madness. His jaw twitched. His blood boiled. His reflection in the glass showed a man haunted—not just by a ghost, but by a woman who wore the ghost like perfume.

Catherine.

Sweet. Smart. Chaotic. Cunning.

Her voice haunted him. Her rejection echoed louder than his own heartbeat.

She didn't want his coffee. She didn't want him.

She didn't even look impressed with the way his coat swayed in the wind like a K-drama villain.

She smiled and laughed like she was untouchable. Like he was the joke.

Worse—she was playing him. Just like Leon.

And so, Alec plotted. With every passing day, he found himself slipping deeper into his own rage, concocting plans to kill him again and again and claim the throne once again. His thoughts grew darker, fed by whispers from a malevolent force—an ancient god of war, murmuring promises of power and vengeance. His fury began to take on a life of its own, becoming something almost tangible, a sinister presence that fuelled his growing obsession. The darkness in him laughed, a chilling sound that echoed through the silence of the forest.

And he, Alec Darrow, was not a man who liked being played.

"MICK!" he roared, slamming his hand down on the desk so hard the vase shattered, the water staining his last remaining Leon photograph.

Mick entered quickly, chewing gum like this was just another Tuesday.

"Yes, boss?"

"Her apartment. Her sanctuary. Break it. I want it wrecked. No people. Just things. I want her to know I've been there." He stood up slowly, voice low and venomous. "Make it look like chaos kissed her world."

Mick blinked. "Like… petty vengeance?"

"Like message received." Alec said, eyes gleaming. "She thinks this is a game. Let's remind her who owns the board."

Soon, it would be the bitch's turn to suffer, to experience the wrath of the man she had tried to mould and control. He envisioned a future where Catherine lay broken, her little house crumbling as he ascended to the throne of winning this little game they play. He wanted more than just revenge; he wanted to watch as the very foundations of her power trembled and fell. The rage within him felt infinite, a vast, untamed force that would not be quelled until he held the title of a champion.

And when that day came, Alec knew he would feel nothing but satisfaction, for he had finally embraced the monster within again, just like what he did to Leon, his brother.

Later That Day

The sun had long since dipped behind a haze of grey. The streets were wet from a surprise drizzle, making everything glisten under the warm hue of streetlamps. My red boots echoed in the stairwell as I carried two bags—one full of discounted bath bombs, the other full of emergency chocolate and cereal. Jaya was now with Mylene for the night.

I unlocked the door, humming under her breath. Then I stepped inside.

Silence. What the heck?

My breath caught. The hallway was dark, too quiet. Something felt off. The scent of lavender cleaner was gone—replaced by cold, bitter air. My boots crunched.

Glass. Chaos. I froze. My eyes scanned the living room. *Destruction.* A shiver ran down my spine. I wanted to look away, to shut it all out, but I couldn't. I was trapped in this vision, forced to witness their exchange, to understand the depths of their madness and his twisted plans of being petty.

The couch cushions had been slashed. My photos torn, frames shattered, glass like snow across the floor. The new smart TV had been knocked over, my books dumped, spines twisted. The kitchen was worse. Every cupboard hung open. My plates were smashed. My favourite coffee mug—Catherine's mug—lay cracked in two, like someone had stomped it in rage.

My heart thudded in my ears. I moved cautiously to the bedroom.

Even worse. My vanity mirror was broken, lipstick smeared across it in a crude X. My clothes were thrown everywhere, drawers gutted like a thief had been searching—except nothing was stolen. It was a storm made of spite. An attack made of *hate and pettiness.*

And on my pillow, carefully placed: *A single shard of the mirror.*

I stood still. No screams. No tears. Just a cold realization. "The *bastard* did this."

My hands curled into fists. Alec had thrown a tantrum like a six-year-old with a God complex. Because I said no. Because I smiled in his face and fed him confusion with a croissant on the side.

"What a child," I muttered, stepping over my broken lamp. I picked up the cracked photo of me and the kids at the park, gently brushing glass from it. My face in the photo smiled. Still whole. I would not cry. Leon never cries.

Instead, I reached for my phone. Dialled a number. "Hello?" Jhing-Jhing answered with her usual chaos in the background.

"He wrecked my place."

"…is the washing machine, okay?"

"Don't joke. I'm serious. He destroyed everything. It's like a rom-com met a horror movie."

Then Mylene's voice in the background: "Did he leave a note that said *'Oops'?*"

"No," I said, voice steel. "But I'm going to leave him a message next."

I kicked over a fallen lamp with her foot. "*Phase Seven* has officially begun."

Meanwhile, in Alec's Office

Alec watched the CCTV footage from the building across Catherine's apartment.

He saw her enter. Saw her stop. Saw her freeze.

He saw her shoulders tighten. Her expression blank. He wanted her to cry.

But she didn't. She didn't break. Instead, she stood taller. A slow dread began to bloom in his chest.

"Sir?" Mick asked.

Alec didn't answer. He stared at the screen, jaw tight. The ghost he thought he could control just looked straight into the lens—like she knew.

Like she could see him. And she smiled. Like a lioness. Like Leon. And Alec, for the first time in years, felt afraid.

Chapter 27

That morning, the sun barely peeked through the clouds like it, too, was unsure whether today would be a good idea. But I knew. I already had plans. Big ones.

I sipped hot chocolate from my new *My Little Pony* plastic mug, clad in pink but not torn pyjamas covered in little ducks wearing sunglasses. Very intimidating. Very war-ready.

I called Joe Smith with calm, surgical precision. The kind of call that sets entire empires on fire. "Joe," I said sweetly, "how about we show Alec that Catherine might be a mother of three, but she's not someone you piss off?"

By 9 a.m., Alec's imported goods from Brazil—silk, cigars, precious stones? Gone. Luxury cars? Missing from the garage. Diamond from his safe? Vanished like a teenage boy's dignity at prom. By noon, his special weapons shipment meant for the Russians was *poof*, re-routed and redirected into military lockdown in a neutral country.

By the afternoon, three luxury shipments meant for Dubai sheikhs—yes, the kind with gold teeth and oil money—were sitting in Korean and Chinese customs, completely stripped of documentation. Angry phone calls roared from the East like sandstorms in a hurricane.

Promises of blood. Demands for explanation. And Alec? He couldn't point fingers at me.

Because I was just Catherine. A friend of Leon. A grieving, overfed widow mom with good taste in snacks and sass.

While Alec's world caught fire behind closed doors, I was having *retail therapy*.

I picked up Mylene and Jhing-Jhing in my SUV. Mylene wore a leopard-print coat that screamed "subtle" like a chainsaw in a chapel. Jhing-Jhing had her hair in a half-bun and baby Ivy strapped to her back like a fashionable ticking time bomb.

"Ladies," I said, sliding my card into the luxury mall's glass doors, "Today we reclaim dignity."

First stop: furniture. The place smelled of cedar, arrogance, and overpriced Scandinavian lighting. I bought couches big enough to swallow sorrow and a crystal coffee table so sharp I could do surgery on it. Flower vases, because I felt like it. Painting of some unknown artist that screams of poignant regrets.

Next: appliances. A talking fridge that could remind me to get revenge. A washing machine that would shame me if I forgot to do laundry. Smart TV. Oven the size of the sun went dark. A pink microwave because vengeance should sparkle.

While the saleslady showed me a marble sink, Jaya tugged at my leg. "Mommy, can I have a rainbow bed that glows?"

Maya asked for everything that glitters. Aliya asked for something dark that screamed murder.

"Sure, baby," I said, adding it to the list. "If Alec's going to act like a gremlin, we deserve to live like royalty."

Jhing Jhing bought a self-cleaning oven she didn't need. Mylene bought wine coolers and matching toasters. "In case Alec comes over again, I'll toast his brain," she said cheerfully.

We bought rugs. Curtains. A chandelier shaped like a phoenix. We even bought matching robes—hot pink with golden embroidery that read

"#TraumaButMakeItFashion."

By late afternoon, we stopped for Korean BBQ and mocktails served in skull-shaped glasses. Jaya dropped lettuce in my purse. Aliya and Maya talked about Korean singers like their life revolved around fake nose and too white skin. Ivy threw a kimchi slice at a man in a suit. The waiter clapped.

"I feel like a rich divorcée from a telenovela," Mylene sighed.

I leaned back, sipping dragon fruit soda. "You should. You're about to be in headlines."

Meanwhile, Alec's phone must've exploded with crisis calls. The sheikh's men were screaming. The Russians cutting ties. His accountant had a meltdown. And still… he wouldn't suspect me.

Because all the trails pointed nowhere. Catherine? She was busy buying a fridge that made smoothies and massaged oiled tofu.

And when Alec tried to track where the rerouting came from, Joe Smith sent a looped security feed of Leon—just Leon—signing off documents a decade ago. Untraceable. Beautifully chaotic.

That night, as the moon grinned like a co-conspirator, I lounged on my new Italian sofa in a velvet robe, drinking tea from a golden mug.

"Mess with my house?" I muttered, flipping through a catalogue for more chandeliers. "I'll ruin yours. With glitter and a goddamn smile."

And somewhere in his mansion, Alec stared at a burning laptop screen, his temples throbbing, screaming at Mick—

"Find out who the hell did this!"

And Mick?

Mick just whispered, "But... was it, Leon?"

Oh Alec, you beautiful idiot. You should've never killed me.

Now you're dating his ghost. It had been a quiet few weeks. *Too* quiet. The kind of silence that made even the walls nervous. Alec hadn't sent a single "accidental" text, hadn't tried to spy, hadn't even sent one of his creepy gifts like that one time he mailed a Chanel bag with a single red rose inside and a note that said *"Regret smells like you."*

Nothing.

Radio silence.

I knew where he was though. The desert. Dubai. Probably busy kissing the Sheik's feet and trying not to cry under his $2,000 sunglasses. And trust me, those Sheikhs? They don't forget. Nor forgive. I imagined him out there, sweating through his designer blazer, haunted by sandstorms and his terrible decision-making. He's probably wandering the dunes like a giraffe out from the snow mountain—confused, lost, and strangely tall for no reason. Whatever that means.

And me?

Oh, I was thriving.

Gym. Yes. The place of pain, sweat, and people who look like they've eaten nothing but quinoa and resentment for five years. But boy, it felt good. I was back. I had lost fifteen pounds, and let me tell you, abs were trying to say hello again, one confused muscle at a time.

The mirror started to respect me again. I caught myself flexing while brushing my teeth and winking at my own reflection like, *"Hey you... yeah, you dangerous spaghetti."*

Then—boom.

At 3AM, just when I was dreaming of Idris Elba feeding me strawberries and affirmations, the door banged. *I mean it was Catherine who dreamed, not me, the Legendary Leon. No that's really ew!*

Not knocked. Banged. Like a drunk gorilla trying to enter a bank. I jolted awake, hair looking like a sad haystack, pyjama shorts twisted like I had fought a wind god. I grabbed my pink glitter slipper like it was a weapon and tiptoed to the door like a cartoon ninja.

Opened it.

There he was.

Ray. The husband. Smelling like vomit, lost dreams, and three kinds of regrets. His shirt was unbuttoned halfway, revealing a belly that looked like it had seen better days. His eyes were bloodshot, his breath could melt paint, and he was swaying like he was dancing to music only he could hear.

"Ba—babe," he slurred, grinning, arms wide. "I missed you."

I blinked. "It's 3AM. Are you drunk?"

"Nooo," he said, tripping over the doormat. "I'm just… spiritually hydrated."

Before I could slam the door, the kids appeared like summoned demons.

"DADDY!"
"Yay, dad's here!"

Suddenly, it was a Disney reunion scene. Hugs. Laughter. Jaya climbed up his leg like a monkey. Maya asked if he brought cake. He didn't. Obviously. Aliya just raised her brow like a drama queen.

I stood there, clutching my glittery slipper, dead inside. After the kids calmed down and went back to sleep—bless their souls—I sat him down on the couch that I had just bought with blood money and revenge.

"I want a divorce," I said simply, voice calm, tone ice-cold. He blinked. Then blinked again, like I had just told him I was moving to Mars with Elon Musk.

"No."

"Excuse me?"

"I don't want a divorce," he said. "I still love you."

I let out a laugh so dry, the Sahara filed a copyright claim. "You still love me? Ray, you disappeared for almost a year. Left me with kids, debt, and a laundry machine that sings 'Despacito' every time I press rinse."

I am Leon, the drama queen.

He looked confused. "I was figuring stuff out..."

"While figuring out how many tequila shots you can survive before face-planting into some stranger's bathroom tiles?"

His face hardened. "I want to come back. I'll take the kids if I have to."

I snapped.

"Oh no, you won't. If you even think about taking those kids—my babies—I will end you."

He stood. "You can't stop me. I'm their father."

I stood too. All 5'4" of rage, motherly wrath, and protein shakes. "Oh Ray," I said sweetly, pulling a spoon from the mug I had just used. "If you ever come back here uninvited again, I will stab you with a spoon and write *I told you so* with a pen on your forehead while you sleep."

He blinked. The room froze. A fly paused mid-air. The fridge stopped humming.

Even the neighbour's cat stared through the window in fear.

Ray gulped. "You're... crazy."

I smiled wide, like a woman on the brink of becoming a legend. "I'm a mother of three. Of course I'm crazy."

He backed up, tripped over a Lego, and limped out the door like a wounded llama.

I locked the door, exhaled, and turned around.

There, Aliya stood sleepily, holding her teddy bear.

"Mommy, are we still getting the rainbow bed tomorrow?"

"Yes, baby," I said, scooping her up. "And maybe a new daddy if the next one isn't stupid."

From the desert dunes to a living room laced with vengeance and bedtime milk, one thing was clear— This mama, this Leon wasn't messing around. It would've been beautiful if Ray got the hint. But Ray was stupid. The kind of stupid that makes you look at a wall and say, "Damn, that drywall got more brain cells."

Because the very next day—he came back. With flowers. And a stuffed toy. And breath that still smelled like someone had mixed gin, cheap regret, and bad life choices into a smoothie.

He knocked on my door like nothing happened, smiling with chipped pride and one eyebrow that refused to grow back evenly.

"Babe," he said. "Let's talk."

Talk?

I stared at him, dead-eyed, wearing my oversized 'World's Best Mistake' hoodie and fuzzy pink slippers that had seen war. The coffee in my hand was still hot. My soul was not.

"No," I replied, sipping dramatically. "We're done."

He took a step forward. Big mistake.

I didn't wait.

I threw the mug straight at him—not the cup, mind you, the contents—scalding-hot revenge roast straight to the face. He screamed like a banshee in heat.

Then, I kicked him so hard where the sun didn't shine, the entire male population winced telepathically.

He bent over like a folding chair. But I wasn't done. Not today. Not ever.

I punched him so hard, POW! the air left the room and his spirit nearly left his body. He collapsed like a dropped lasagna—sloppy, loud, and embarrassing.

That's when the front door flew open.

"YAAAAS!" Jhing Jhing screamed, standing there like a cheerleader of chaos with a Bluetooth headset on. "She did it! She landed the punch! Mylene—bring popcorn! And the twins! It's go-time!"

And Mylene? She burst in like a Marvel villain in Louboutins holding popcorn, juice boxes, and two screaming toddlers dressed like green Pikachu and a mini-Elon Musk with pink make up.

"Let the record show," she said dramatically, tossing a kernel into her mouth, "that this man deserved it."

Ray, lying there with one eye open and half his soul disconnected from the Wi-Fi of life, whimpered. Then, the police showed up—again. Our favourite duo: Officer Marko, who lowkey had a crush on Jhing Jhing, and Officer Lizal, who never smiled unless someone got arrested.

They looked at me. Looked at Ray.

Saw the bruises. Saw the mess.

Officer Mark shrugged. "He drunk again?"

"Like a fermented goat," I said.

"Alright, in the car, sir," Officer Lizal said, slapping cuffs on Ray like it was her cardio routine. "Don't cry. You did this to yourself."

As they dragged him out, I handed him a neatly folded stack of divorce papers. Fresh. Legal. Ruthless.

"I've had this ready for weeks," I said. "It has tabs and everything."

"I've changed," he croaked. "You'll see…"

"I did see," I said coldly, "and I chose violence."

He didn't sign it. Of course he didn't. He promised again. Vowed to "be better." To "win me back." To "stop mixing gin with sadness."

But fate said, no thanks.

Because the next day—bam.

News broke.

Chapter 28

Ray… was hit by a truck. A big one. With a sticker that read: *"Honk if you love karma."*

I was livid. Not because he died. But because he died before signing the damn papers.

Now I was stuck organizing a burial for a man I didn't even like. And of course, the universe had a sense of drama because it rained. Heavily. Like a scene from a sad indie movie no one wanted.

People showed up. Cried fake tears. One relative tried to hit on me while I held an umbrella. Another aunt accused me of turning Ray gay (he wasn't, just stupid).

I stood there, under the storm clouds, mascara intact, looking every bit like a widow from a telenovela who secretly owned a yacht full of secrets.

And then, it was over. We went back home. To my apartment. To my girls. And we partied. I mean *full-blown celebration.*

There was karaoke, champagne, juice boxes, fried chicken, a shirtless man named Brun who Jhing Jhing hired for "emotional support," and a surprise visit from the chaos twins who tied balloons to my ceiling fan and made it snow glitter.

We danced. We laughed. Someone (me) peed a little while laughing too hard during Maya's "Ray was a Cockroach" song.

And that night, as the city lights blinked outside and laughter echoed through my living room, I whispered to myself—

"I am Leon Darrow. I am death. I am the destroyer."

And the world, my darling, had just been warned.

Then came Thanksgiving. The only thing I knew about it was: It involved turkey and hidden eggs. People cry and give thanks for stuff they secretly hate.

Pilgrims? Maybe? Or gifts exchanged.

There's pie. Many pies. Possibly a cult?

I don't celebrate Thanksgiving.

I celebrate more important things. Like the day I rerouted gold from Mongolia to the Philippines and personally greeted it in heels and a power suit while the customs officer cried out of confusion and awe. Now *that* was a holiday. But here in the land of suburban expectations and grocery wars, I was a fish out of gravy. The whole country suddenly acted like roasted birds were sacred gods and mashed potatoes could fix generational trauma and more regrets.

So naturally, I called Mylene. And thank the gods of housewives, her husband, cancelled coming back home from Afghanistan.

Because if anyone knew how to out-shop a midlife crisis and cook a turkey big enough to feed both our enemies and their mothers, it was her.

She showed up wearing sunglasses indoors, pushing a cart like it was a Formula One car. "We need a turkey the size of Alec's ego," she declared, already tossing things into the cart like she was in a televised supermarket sweep.

Me? I was clueless.

"What's a giblet?" I asked, staring at a package that looked like organ donation leftovers.

"Don't ask. Just throw it in," she said. "We'll make someone's uncle eat it."

And so, we began our shopping spree.

Three carts. Two kids per cart. Maya and Aliya behind us, still talking about BTS and Roblox and the latest TikTok meme. Jaya was chewing on a cinnamon-scented pinecone. Mylene's twin was asleep inside a box of instant stuffing. One was wearing a rotisserie chicken hat and the other kept licking the freezer aisle door and claiming it tasted like dreams.

We got everything on her list. A list so long it could be used to suffocate a small man.

A turkey so huge we needed a forklift. Seven pies, none of which were the same flavour. Sweet potatoes that could kill someone if thrown. Enough greens to make a vegan weep. Several bottles of wine because we're not saints. And a table runner that read *"Gobble You C*nt Now!"* which we bought ironically but secretly loved.

At some point, a man tried to steal our cart. Mylene hissed at him like a cat and he backed off. The chaos twins threw a can of cranberry sauce at his foot just in case.

An employee tried to ask if we needed help, but once he saw Mylene lifting a frozen turkey like a kettlebell while yelling at the kids in three languages, he turned around and walked the other way.

Me? I just kept looking around thinking:

"Is this what people do for one meal? One turkey dinner? This feels like a military operation. I've smuggled diamonds with less effort."

But I have to admit, despite the madness, the aisles filled with screaming toddlers, glittery pumpkin decor, and seventeen versions of gravy mix— I felt... kind of good. Strong. Ready. Armed with carts full of carbs and vengeance.

As we rolled up to the checkout, Mylene high-fived me.

"This," she said with pride, "is the kind of feast you throw when you've survived a dead husband, a mafia ex-stalker, and a blackmail attempt by the Russian mob."

I laughed, nearly ran over a display of cranberry juice, and whispered to myself:

"I still don't know what Thanksgiving really is... But I do know we're about to make this holiday our bitch."

Then came the cooking.

The kind of chaos that could only be described as *culinary warfare with a splash of telenovela*. The battlefield? My newly redecorated pink kitchen.

The weapons? A 25-pound turkey, Jhing Jhing's emotional instability, and three women with enough trauma to season a thousand meals.

Jhing Jhing showed up with her arms full of groceries and her mouth full of complaints.

"I miss my old oven," she said dramatically, slamming a bag of garlic on the counter. "It used to talk to me. Literally. It told me, 'Dinner is ready, darling.' This one? Silent. Cold. Emotionally unavailable. Like my ex."

She threw a cabbage at the counter. It bounced off and hit the wall.

"And my new maid!" she yelled, flinging her arms in the air like a telenovela villain. "She wore leggings so tight her camel toe was crying for help in Morse code. And my husband had the nerve to *grin*. Grin! I almost served him a knuckle sandwich for breakfast."

Mylene, stirring something suspiciously creamy, didn't even flinch. "Just fire her."

"I did. She cried. I cried. Then I Venmo'd her a bonus and told her to leave before I set her leggings on fire."

Meanwhile, the kids were not around—thank every known deity and minor saint. They were at the park being watched by three Filipina maids we'd temporarily employed for the day. Professional, unbothered, and immune to toddler screams, those women were the true

MVPs of the Thanksgiving prep. I was planning to build them a statue later.

Back in the kitchen, we began fighting the turkey.

The thing was massive. It could've been its own country. Mylene tried to shove garlic butter under its skin like it owed her the world.

Jhing Jhing tried to brine it using a bucket and accidentally dropped the bucket.

I stabbed it with rosemary like I was purging it of its past sins.

We sweated.

We yelled. We laughed maniacally while covered in poultry juice and butter. It was gross and glorious.

Meanwhile, Jhing Jhing's true calling emerged. While Mylene and I were still trying to find out how to make pie crusts not feel like cardboard regret, she quietly cooked up chicken adobo.

And I kid you not—it tasted like *heaven and sex had a baby and raised it in a garlic spa*. I took one bite and nearly moaned. "If I wasn't already divorced, I'd marry this chicken."

Jhing Jhing raised her spoon like a weapon. "You're welcome. Generations of heartbreak and soy sauce went into that."

As the smells filled the air—turkey roasting like a juicy trophy, pie bubbling like sweet betrayal, adobo simmering like poetry—I had a moment. A strange, still moment in the middle of the madness.

I stood there, wearing a gravy-stained apron, my hair up with a kitchen tong, a kid's drawing stuck to my back somehow, and I just thought:

"I could almost swear... I'm becoming Catherine."

Not just pretending. Not just hiding. But actually, becoming her. I laughed easier now. Cried when I wanted. I wore soft cardigans instead of bulletproof vests. I argued over stuffing, not smuggling routes. I hugged my friends instead of threatening rivals.

And yes, it scared me. Because for so long, being Leon Darrow meant control, strategy, power. It meant surviving. But this—cooking with friends, yelling at pies, laughing over garlic—this felt like living. A part of me mourned Leon. He was brutal, brilliant, and dangerously cool. But a louder part whispered:

"Leon never felt this alive."

Not even when he outsmarted billionaires. Not even when he held entire cities in his pocket. Not even when he rerouted Mongolian gold through three continents while sipping espresso in a bathrobe.

So yes... Thanksgiving? Still weird. Still confusing. But as I stared at that turkey—golden, sizzling, majestic—I realized something else:

I was happy. Really happy. And that scared me even more than the camel toe maid.

*****

Then came dinner—that glorious, chaotic, movie-worthy moment of truth. The front door opened and in marched the three Filipina babysitters, dragging in our sugar-high, giggling children like war prisoners of cuteness. The women looked like they'd just walked out of a live-action warzone. Their hair was frizzed, clothes askew, eyes wild. One of them whispered something in Tagalog that suspiciously sounded like a prayer.

Still, they delivered the kids with only one scraped knee, one missing shoe, and a whole lot of psychological damage. We saluted them in silence. They didn't even wait for a tip—just nodded grimly, muttering "God bless," like trained mercenaries who knew when to retreat.

The turkey, however, was a triumph. Golden. Glorious. Smelling like redemption and buttery lust. We carved it with reverence and served it like an offering to the gods of carbs and calories. The chicken adobo shined beside it like the seductive side character in a K-drama. The pies—still lopsided—tasted like sweet trauma and burnt effort.

Then came the dancing.

Oh, the dancing.

We started with music. Then came the karaoke, which no one asked for and everyone regretted. I—me, once the kingpin of silence and precision—grabbed the mic and murdered a Mariah Carey song so violently the turkey nearly came back to life to file a noise complaint. I shrieked. I howled. I hit notes that hadn't been invented.

Mylene, drunk off her third mimosa and a suspiciously strong "apple cider," danced like her knees were made of Play-Doh and her soul had gone to Ibiza.

She twerked in front of the refrigerator. She grinded on a chair. She tried to slap Jhing Jhing's butt but missed and hit a pie.

The children, now bloated with sugar, ran in circles. We fed them sweets and diabetes like irresponsible yet well-meaning aunts. One of them licked the wall. No one stopped them.

Jun, Jhing's poor husband, came to "check in."

He stepped into the room, took in the sight—Mylene fake crying on the karaoke mic, Jhing Jhing belly laughing with a meat skewer in hand, and me dancing with a child's tiara on my head—and silently turned around with his plate and left. He knew better.

We partied hard.

Too hard.

The next morning? Armageddon.

The kitchen looked like a post-apocalyptic battlefield. Bottles everywhere. Half-eaten pie. A lollipop and vomit shared the same corner like two unfortunate roommates.

The turkey carcass sat like a fallen hero.

The TV was still playing karaoke tracks in the background, echoing trauma.

The three Filipina babysitters were gone. Not a trace. Probably escaped at dawn and left us to rot. I wouldn't blame them. I'd have left too.

Mylene was once again under the table, hugging a bottle of sparkling water like it owed her money. She groaned and hissed at the light like a vampire who'd seen too much.

I woke up in the bathroom, face planted on a Hello Kitty bath mat, wearing someone else's robe and one sock. I groaned, sat up, saw my reflection and screamed internally.

The kids were all in the master bedroom, cuddled together in what looked like a cuddle-puddle of sugar crashes and dreams. One of them had drawn a turkey on the wall in what I prayed was dark chocolate.

We gathered like survivors. Sat around the kitchen, drinking coffee like it was holy water.

We swore—again—we would *never drink like that again*.

But of course, we lied.

Because a few hours later, after a group nap and a round of ibuprofen and leftover pie, I checked my burner phone and received a lovely update from Joe.

Alec had returned from Dubai.

With a bruised ego. An even more bruised pride. And an empty wallet.

Apparently, the sheikh had demanded compensation, and Alec—idiot, overconfident Alec—tried to save face by selling off three properties in one day.

Too bad.

Because Joe, my loyal tech genius with a petty streak and hacker thumbs, had already rerouted the documents. By the time Alec went to finalize, the properties were

gone.
Gone.

Mine now.

Thanks to Joe's lightning-fast fingers, he accidentally sold two of my old mansions in Greece *(I didn't even remember owning those)*, and three townhouses in Scotland and Vegas.

Where did the money go?

Straight to my Swiss account. Untraceable. Invisible. Delicious.

I sipped my black coffee like it was the tears of my enemies and smiled. Because no matter how drunk, how chaotic, how painfully normal life was becoming...

I was still Leon Darrow. Just in fuzzy socks and a tiara.

And Alec?

He was now in debt, friendless, emasculated, and living off hotel breakfast bars while begging the market to crash so he could breathe again.

God, I loved Thanksgiving.

Chapter 29

But happiness never stays long. It always walks out the back door just when you're starting to think it's finally unpacked and planning to stay.

And sure enough—the bastard Alec returned like a roach you thought you squashed but somehow crawled back with vengeance in his antennae.

I didn't even know how he was still alive. The man had nothing. His wallet was emptier than my soul on tax season, his men were betraying him left and right, and word on the street said he'd even tried to sell a fake Picasso to an Albanian arms dealer and nearly got his nose broken in the process.

But no. Alec wasn't dead. He was just getting desperate. And stupid.

It started on a Thursday morning. A stupid, sunny, annoyingly perfect Thursday. I was at the gym, aggressively pretending I had muscles to appease. I was in the middle of lifting what felt like a dying elephant disguised as a kettlebell when my phone rang.

Mylene. Her voice came through, shaking, breathless, barely even a whisper:

"He was at the school, Cathy. Alec. He was asking around about... Maya and Aliya."

I froze.

Everything in my brain stopped moving. My blood turned cold. My grip on the kettlebell slackened, and it dropped to the floor with a loud, accusing thud.

I didn't even say goodbye.

I just ran. Out of the gym, through the doors, past some guy yelling about me not re-racking my weights. I sprinted to the parking lot, jumped into my SUV, and slammed on the gas so hard I think the tires cried out in pain. I don't remember the traffic; I don't remember the honking—I just remember flying.

When I arrived at the school gate, I saw Mylene crying. Actually crying. Not drunk-crying, not movie-crying—real fear and heartbreak. Her cheeks were streaked. Her hands were trembling. She pointed to the empty space where the security guard was talking on the phone and mouthing "I'm sorry."

And I knew.

My babies were gone.

Maya and Aliya—my sweet, giggling, smart-mouthed girls. My little warriors. My reasons for not burning the world to ash.

Kidnapped.

By him. By Alec.

I think something inside me snapped. I was no longer Catherine. I wasn't even Leon. I was something else entirely. Something that wore human skin but thought like a mother who'd been pushed too far.

I turned to Mylene, my mouth opening to scream, curse, cry—but she just climbed into the SUV and said:

"The kids can stay at my apartment. I'm going with you."

She was panicking. Desperate. She wanted to help. But I couldn't focus. My entire being was set on murder. I nearly forgot they were in the back seat.

We dropped her kids off like a scene from a spy movie—fast, breathless, tight hugs and whispers of "be brave." Mylene gave her kids the kind of look you give before heading into war.

Then we headed to the police station.

I filed the report. I gave every detail. The officers were sympathetic. They promised they'd do everything. But I'd been Leon Darrow long enough to know better.

The police wouldn't find them. I would.

So, while Mylene cried and answered questions, I slipped away and drove straight to the school again.

I found the CCTV room. I bribed the guard with my 24k gold bracelet and a promise of silence. And there he was. Alec. In full view. Wearing a cap. Talking to a staff member. Looking around. Then walking with two girls in hoodies. My girls. They were smiling. He probably lied. Said I was waiting. Said there was a surprise. I wanted to tear the screen in half. I immediately called Joe.

"He took them," I hissed into the line. "Find him. Now. I don't care what it takes."

Joe didn't ask questions. He never did. He just said, "Yes, boss," and I heard his mechanical keyboard clicking like it was out for blood.

We started tracing signals, contacts, back-alley cameras—everything.

Hours passed. My nails were bitten down. Mylene kept pacing, whispering to the gods and every saint she knew.

Still… no news.

Every minute felt like a year. Every hour like a knife twisted in my gut. I couldn't eat. I couldn't sit. I stood in front of the map we drew on the whiteboard in Joe's office, tracking potential locations.

I swore to myself. If I found Alec—no power on this Earth would stop me from ending him.

But then… my phone rang. And I held my breath.

The call came. My heart leapt.

But it wasn't Alec.

It was Jhing Jhing, her voice cracking like glass shattering through the phone. Panicked. Screaming.

"Cath—Catherine! It's Ivy and MJ—they're gone! I— I left them with the new maid for thirty minutes—I just— I went to buy pancit at the corner! And now they're GONE!"

My hand tightened around Jaya, who clung to me like a sleepy little koala, unaware that the world had just cracked open again.

"No, no, no, no, no—" I whispered, holding Jaya tighter, my breath caught between a sob and a scream.

The floor felt like it was slipping beneath me. One minute, it was my girls—now it was Jhing Jhing's. It wasn't just Alec trying to destroy me now—he was targeting my family.

I didn't even hesitate.

I pressed the phone tight to my ear and said, "Listen, Jhing. I need you to go to the police station. Right now. Mylene's coming to get you. You're not doing this alone."

"But—"
"No buts! Go. I swear on everything that still matters in this broken world—I'll bring them back."

I turned to Mylene, eyes fierce, voice shaking, "Go. Now."

She didn't argue. She kissed Jaya on the forehead, grabbed her purse, and ran out like the building was on fire.

And I?

I walked down the quiet hallway of my apartment like a ghost returning to its crypt.

I passed by the kitchen, past the glittering chandelier I stole from a black-market gallery in the mall, past the scattered toys and fallen chairs—straight to my secret room.

The one only Leon Darrow knew existed.

The moment I locked the door behind me, I let it all go.

Rage. Terror. Hatred. Grief.

I stood in front of the mirror, chest heaving, hands shaking, staring at the face that used to belong to someone else. Catherine's soft features, her gentle eyes, her delicate skin.

But inside—inside, I was burning.

I punched the wall.

Hard.

Once. Twice. Over and over until blood ran down my knuckles and the drywall caved in.

I whispered like a mantra:

"I am Leon Darrow.

I am death.

I am the kingpin.

I am the destroyer."

And Alec? He messed with my kids.

With Catherine's kids. And I promised her. When I woke up in her body. When her soul passed on. When her memories filled my heart like warm sunlight before vanishing into dust—I promised her I'd protect them.

And now they were gone.

Tears mixed with the sweat on my face. The hatred coiled inside me like a venomous snake biting its own tail.

I pulled out my old phone. The encrypted one. The one with Joe's private line.

"Joe. It's me."

"Boss. Tell me."

"One million pounds."

Silence.

"For what?"

"Alec's head. Mounted. Delivered. Gift wrapped if you can manage it."

Joe didn't even flinch. "Done."

He didn't ask why. He didn't ask how. He just moved.

Within minutes, I saw the digital red light on the wall blink twice. A signal.

Joe had launched the hit.

London. Berlin. Dubai. Bangkok. Our network was wide and relentless.

I stared at the cracked mirror. Blood dripping down my wrist. Jaya's stuffed bunny lay on the ground where I'd dropped it.

"You won't win this time, Alec," I whispered, lips curling into a snarl. "You won't touch them again. You won't live long enough to try."

Because this time, Leon Darrow wasn't playing gangster.

This time, he was playing god.

Few hours passed.

They felt like ticking time bombs strapped to my spine—every second dragging, humming, aching with dread. No word. No update. No Joe. No police.

No Maya. No Aliya. No Ivy. No MJ.

And then—

The phone rang. I stared at the screen, my heart thudding like a war drum. No caller ID. Just a dark, dead number.

I answered. "Hello?"

Laughter. Thick. Mocking. Cruel.

It filled the line like smoke choking out the air. "Ohhhh, Catherine... darling, *or should I say Leon?*"

Chapter 30

I froze. Every hair on my body stood on end.

"Surprised? Come on. I knew something was off the second you walked out of that casino with my money and my pride. You move like him. Think like him. Bleed like him. The cold stare. The damn smile. And those impossible wins—nobody does that but Leon Darrow."

He was laughing, but it was the laugh of a man unravelling.

"You've been screwing with me, haven't you?" he hissed. "You're the one who stole my properties. Who ruined the Dubai deal. Who turned my men. YOU—Leon. YOU came back in that pretty little dress and you made me a clown."

I screamed his name, my voice hoarse, my throat burning:

"WHERE ARE MY KIDS?!"

There was silence.

Then—

A faint noise. Children. Crying. A scream. Maya. Aliya. Another scream. Then a *slap*.

"NO!" I roared into the phone, my whole soul leaving my lungs. "TOUCH THEM AND I'LL—"

Shut up," Alec said coldly. "You want them back? Come alone. No Joe. No Mylene. No Jhing Jhing. Just you."

I didn't even need to hear the location.

Because then he said the words I expected.

"Meet me at the old cabin. The one up the mountain. The one that's hidden so well not even the government satellites can find it. Your little hideout, right Leon?"

And then the call cut.

The phone slipped from my fingers like dead weight.

My cabin. The one I built when I was still Leon. Carved into the rocks of the mountain like a second spine. Camouflaged, self-sustaining, lined with emergency weapons, escape hatches, and trauma kits.

It was meant to be a fortress. And now Alec was using it against me.

But I smiled. Because he didn't know what I'd buried in that cabin. He didn't know that every plank of wood in that place was soaked in secrets and blood.

I picked up a tiny picture.

Of Catherine. With the girls. In the garden. Laughing. I stared at it and whispered, "I'll bring them back. I swear."

I threw on a black jacket, tied my hair, and hid the gear under the seats of my SUV. Tossed a blanket over the weapons.

I was going camping. But more than that?

I was going killing. I didn't need the police.

I didn't need backup. I was Leon Darrow.

And I was bringing hell with me.

Then came another call. Jhing Jhing's kids. Ivy and MJ. Alex had them too.

The silence after the call was louder than the scream I let out.

Now, I stood in the middle of the room again, phone still in my hand, knuckles white, jaw clenched so tightly it felt like my teeth would snap. The laughter—Alec's laughter—still echoed in my ears. The way he said *Leon*. The way he mocked me. The way the children cried in the background.

I sank to the floor, forehead against my knees, trying to breathe, but every inhale felt like glass in my lungs. I wasn't just angry. I wasn't just terrified. I was *violently unravelling*. And all I could see was Maya and Aliya, my girls, terrified… hurt… alone.

And Ivy and MJ. Jhing Jhing's babies. Sweet, giggly, innocent. They were probably clinging to each other, too scared to understand why.

Alec took our babies. The man had lost everything—his pride, his empire, his damn sense of reality—and now he wanted blood to feel powerful again. He wanted *me*.

He wanted Leon.

I stood up.

No. Not stood.

Rose.

Like a storm. Like a plague. Like something ancient that should've stayed buried.

I went to the bedroom. Quietly. Jaya was asleep on the bed, arms wrapped around a unicorn plushie. The Filipina maid I hired just hours ago was dozing lightly in the armchair. She stirred when I stepped inside, blinking.

"Ma'am?"

I knelt beside her and whispered, "Stay with her. Don't open the door for anyone but Jhing Jhing or Mylene. Got it?"

She nodded quickly.

Good girl.

Now...let's play no more games. I left with a dark shirt that says "Because you don't have to be everyone's cup of tea. Be gasoline. Set shit on fire."

Ten minutes later, I was in my secret room again after yet another call from Alec. I know he was playing. He wanted me so badly that it pained him to not even hear my voice. He wanted Leon and Catherine so bad.

Yes, *the* room. The one behind the bookcase, where Leon's world still lived in shadows. The scent of gun oil and old secrets still clung to the walls. A shelf hidden behind my dresses swung open when I pressed the hidden tile beneath the rug.

I hadn't used this room in months. But tonight... Tonight it welcomed me back like an old friend. I opened the floor hatch and pulled out the duffel bag. It wasn't just a bag. It was an oath. Inside were items I swore I'd never touch again.

Glock 17. Fully loaded. No serials. Silencer in the side pocket.

Twin boot knives. Silver-plated. Razor sharp. One engraved with the word "HUSH."

Duct tape. Taser. Zip ties. Tactical gloves. Rope. Satellite phone. Bounced signals off a relay tower I'd built on a trip to Nepal. Alec would never trace it.

Thermal scope. Compact drone. Binoculars.

Chocolate bars. Water. Protein gels. Just enough for the kids if I needed to keep moving.

Cyanide pill. Just in case.

Taped to the underside of the duffel was a photograph. It wasn't recent. It was old, creased, and smudged.
Catherine. The real Catherine. Sitting in the park with the girls on her lap. Her hair was in a messy bun. The sun caught her dimples. The girls were laughing.

I stared at it for a long time. My throat burned. "I promised you I'd take care of them," I whispered. "And I keep my promises."

I locked the apartment behind me, walked down the dim hallway of the apartment like a ghost, and stepped into the underground parking. My SUV—armoured, upgraded, GPS-shielded—waited like a loyal dog.

I tossed the bag into the back seat and gunned the engine. I drove like the road was mine and the law didn't exist. The GPS blinked silently. I didn't need it. I knew that mountain. I built my first empire up there.

But before I hit the highway, I pulled over to make a single call.

To Joe.

He picked up instantly.

"Boss?"

"I want him dead," I growled. "Sniper. Mercenary. Clean hit. I want his body on a plate or scattered in the wind. I don't care how."

There was silence on the line.

Then: "It's done."

He didn't ask why. Joe never needed to.

"Also," I added, "Scramble surveillance on the mountain. I'm going in. Alone. If I don't come out, burn the place down."

"Understood. Godspeed."

The mountain loomed in the distance like a grave.

Snow clung to its craggy slopes like the hands of the dead. The sun had long since sunk below the horizon, and dusk bled into full night, painting the world in cold steel. Up there, in the darkness, hidden beneath the pines and silence, waited the bastard who betrayed me.

Alec.

It would be his grave soon. And I'd be the one to carve his name into the soil with a bullet.

I didn't tell Jhing. I didn't tell Mylene. They thought I was coordinating with the police, waiting for news.

But Alec had already called me again. His voice still crawled under my skin like maggots in rot. His laughter. The way he said my name—Leon—with such venom. As if I was the intruder in my own body.

He demanded I come alone.

And I would.

But I wasn't alone.

Catherine was with me.

She was *always* with me now.

In the twitch of my fingers, in the feral thrum of my heartbeat, in the tears I couldn't explain, and the rage I no longer wanted to control.

We weren't separate anymore. Not truly.

Her fury burned inside me like kerosene on a slow drip.

And now…now I wasn't going to the gym to pretend I had control.

I was going to kill the bastard who took our children.

Chapter 31

The fog thickened the farther I drove up the winding path, curling around the SUV like smoke from a battlefield. The trees lined the road like soldiers standing at silent attention. The headlights cut swaths of light through the mist, illuminating patches of gravel, half-frozen puddles, the scattered claw marks of passing animals.

Above, the moon was a slit behind the clouds, pale and cold. Snow had begun to fall—light, scattered flakes that melted against the windshield but whispered promises of more to come.

The air was sharp, biting, laced with pine and something else. Something older. Something wrong.

Alec's madness clung to this place now.

And I was mad, too.

But not in the way he thought.

He took Maya and Aliya. He took Ivy and MJ. He didn't just provoke me—he awoke something inside me I had buried with Leon's ashes.

A darkness. A precision. A hunger for vengeance that no amount of justice could satisfy. This wasn't about money, or status, or empire anymore. This wasn't about the billion-dollar casino, or the art collection, or the underworld crown.

He took the only thing that mattered to me in this life.

And now I was bringing everything I had.

Few hours later, the road turned from asphalt to gravel and finally to ice-crusted mud. I killed the lights, letting the SUV roll into a quiet stop. Silence swallowed the forest. I stepped out, my boots crunching against snow-laced gravel. The cold slapped me in the face like a warning, but I didn't flinch.

I threw the duffel over my shoulder, double-checked my weapons, and pulled the hood of my tactical jacket over my head. Wind howled between the trees—low and guttural, like the mountain itself was mourning what was about to come.

This was no longer a mountain. It was a tomb.

I moved through the trees like a shadow—silent, deliberate. The terrain here was familiar to me. The slope dropped into a ravine to the left, sharp rocks and ice lining the edge. To the right, a steep climb covered in pine and snowdrifts. I stuck to the old deer trail, now barely visible beneath the white, my boots sinking softly with each step.

Every creak of a branch. Every rustle of wind. Every crunch of snow.

All of it sharpened my senses, but none of it scared me. Only one thing scared me now—failing to bring them home.

I'd failed once before. I failed when Alec stole my empire. I failed when I died.

No more failures. I reached the clearing just past midnight.

The cabin stood at the centre like a beast squatting in the dark. Two stories. Log structure. Hidden cellar. Reinforced doors. Motion sensors—disabled now. Probably by Alec himself.

The snow around it was undisturbed. Too clean. Too perfect. A trap waiting to be sprung.

But he didn't know I had eyes. I crouched low behind a tree, pulled out the drone, and launched it with a soft hum. It rose like a ghost above the clearing, its camera feeding into my phone.

Thermal signatures bloomed across the screen.

Two upstairs. Smaller. Children. Huddled together.

One downstairs. Alone. Alec. Kitchen, probably. Where the whiskey was. Or the knives. He was waiting. I watched him on the screen, pacing slowly. He was agitated. Moving like a cornered dog who thought he still had teeth.

I smiled. That bastard had no idea what was coming. I slid the drone back into the bag, unslung the rifle from my back, and chambered a round.

You took the wrong kids, Alec. I whispered one last thing to the wind. "I'm coming for you." Then I moved toward the cabin like the storm I had become.

And I brought death with me. The snow swallowed my footsteps as I circled the cabin's perimeter, every breath crystallizing in the air like whispered ghosts. The wind howled above the treetops, slicing through the pines, carrying the weight of all the lives Alec and I had burned through.

The thermal map burned behind my eyes.

Two small signatures upstairs. The kids. Alive.

But cold. Still. Huddled. I could almost hear Maya's tiny sobs. Aliya's defiance. They were their mother's daughters. They would hold on.

The cabin itself hadn't changed—same wood paneling, same rusted weather vane creaking on the roof, same back door that looked locked but always had a weakness under the hinge.

Alec never learned that trick. That was mine. I crouched in the snow by the north wall, exhaled once, and reached for my radio.

"Joe," I whispered, voice a low growl.

A faint crackle answered.

"Boss."

"Status?"

"Snipers are 300 meters south. No visual on hostiles outside. We're blind beyond that."

"Stay out of sight. No shots unless I say. He wants me alone. Let's keep that illusion alive."

"Understood."

I clicked the radio off. This was personal. And I needed Alec to know that.

Inside the cabin I slipped in through the back like smoke, moving past the darkened pantry, across the cold stone tiles of the kitchen. The place reeked of old wood, blood, and brandy. A fireplace crackled in the main room. Shadows danced on the walls. One chair. One table. One bottle, half-empty.

Alec was there.

Sitting, back to me, sipping a glass of amber liquid. Not a care in the world.

"You're late," he said, without turning.

My fingers tightened around the grip of my pistol, but I didn't raise it. Not yet.

"You were always better at being early," he continued. "Planning. Manipulating. Watching. But showing up? No, Catherine. That was never your strong suit."

He turned slowly.

He looked older now. Gaunt. Paranoid. A man torn apart by years of losing. His left eye was bruised; a long scar now marred the corner of his lip. But his smile remained. Twisted. Feral.

And familiar.

"Or should I say... Leon?" He chuckled at his own joke, tilting his head like a dog mocking its master.

"You really are him, aren't you?" he asked, eyes gleaming. "The way you scream. The way you fight. You think I didn't notice? The eyes.. The temper. The perfume."

"You talk too much," I said.

"Ah, there he is." He leaned forward. "The killer king himself. But you're not fooling anyone, brother. You're still Catherine underneath. Still the mama who had heart failure. Scared of her husband."

I moved closer, slow, silent. Letting the fury settle deep in my bones. Letting his words slice into the places I kept hidden.

"You don't get to say her name," I whispered.

He laughed. "Oh, come on. I should thank you. You gave me everything. Your empire. Your women. Your secrets. And now... your daughters? Huh! Catherine's legacy. Tell me—"

He leaned back, swirling his drink. "Did you really think you could keep something pure? Something untouched? After all we did? After all you did? You made me this way brother."

My hand twitched on the trigger.

"I swear to God," I said, voice low, "if you hurt them—"

"Oh, they're fine," Alec said with a shrug. "A little cold. A little scared. But alive. For now."

His gaze sharpened.

"But here's the thing, Catherine... Leon... whatever the hell you are now—what's it like? Living in her skin? Feeling her thoughts? Did it break you? Or did it set you free?"

I stepped closer until I was only a few feet away. Close enough to smell the sweat on his shirt. The cheap scotch on his breath.

"You want to know what it's like?" I said quietly.

He leaned forward.

I leaned closer.

"It's like fire," I said. "It's like every scream she held back burns in my blood now. Every bruise she endured. Every lie you fed her. I carry it all."

I pulled out the small blade and pressed it to the table.

"But most of all… I carry her promise."

He narrowed his eyes.

"What promise?"

"That I would end you."

His hand moved toward his belt.

Too slow.

I kicked the table hard—it smashed into his knees. He howled, fell back, and I was on him before he could recover. We tumbled to the floor, fists flying. The scotch bottle shattered beside us.

He grabbed a shard and slashed at my arm—pain tore through the sleeve, but I didn't stop.

This wasn't just a fight. It was a reckoning.

For Maya.
For Aliya.
For Catherine.
For me.

He scrambled back toward the stairs, blood on his lip. "You won't make it out alive!" he screamed, breath ragged. "You think this ends with me? There are more! I made deals—!"

I drew my pistol and fired once—just above his head. The bullet slammed into the wood behind him. He froze.

"I don't care who you made deals with."

I advanced; pistol raised.

"I came here for my daughters. I came here for Ivy and MJ. I came here to finish your madness."

He laughed again—bloody, bitter.

Even if you kill me, you'll never escape this life. It owns you now."

"I own it now," I said.

Then I shot him.

Not in the head.

Not yet.

In the legs. Both legs. Just to be sure, after all I am a mom. I am Leon.

He dropped like a sack of bones, screaming.

I walked past him, up the stairs. The girls were in the bedroom.

Cold. Scared. But alive.

Maya ran into my arms, crying. "Mommy!" Aliya punched me in the chest, then hugged me.

"Mommy...did you kill that very bad guy?"

Ivy and MJ sobbed behind them.

I held them all. "No, of course not. Killing is bad."

"But he slapped Maya?"

"I've got you; he won't hurt you anymore," I whispered. "You're safe. Mommy's got you."

Outside, the wind howled louder.

And below, Alec screamed into the floorboards.

But no one answered.

Chapter 32

What happened next was blurry. The storm came down like judgment. Thick, blinding sheets of snow slammed against the cabin windows, turning the world outside into a churning white void. Wind screamed through the trees like a chorus of ghosts, and the temperature dropped so fast my breath iced the glass. I knew at that moment—no helicopter was coming tonight. No snowcat. No convoy. Not unless they wanted to die trying.

We were stuck here. In my cabin. In Alec's failed trap.

But this place, this mountain—it belonged to me long before he ever stepped foot on it. And so did everything hidden beneath the floorboards and false walls.

The kids huddled together near the massive stone fireplace, wrapped in thick quilts that smelled like cedar and gun oil. I made a fire quickly— memory from darker years. The flames rose like guardians, painting their faces in flickering gold. Maya clutched her sister. Aliya sat with a quiet tear rolling down her cheek. MJ chewed on the corner of her blanket, too exhausted to cry anymore.

I moved fast. My body on autopilot, driven by something deep—a parent's rage and a soldier's calm. I found the hidden latch near the back wall and pulled it. The groan of metal hinges echoed through the cabin as I lifted the trap door. The cold vault beneath yawned open—a forgotten bunker I built years ago, back when paranoia and dream coexisted like oil and water.

Down there was everything I never trusted banks to hold.

I descended into the earth. The concrete walls dripped with condensation, and the emergency lights flickered weakly, casting shadows that danced like old regrets. But the supplies were untouched.

First, I found the fridge the size of a car, buried under camouflage tarp. Powered by a separate generator. Inside—frozen meats, vegetables, cans of powdered milk, sealed meals from a private army surplus I used to own. Food for years.

The girls would not go hungry. Not tonight. Not ever.

I stocked a basket—chocolate bars, warm milk powder, dried fruits, and bread I'd baked and vacuum-sealed a years ago. Still good. Still soft.

Back upstairs, I boiled water over the fire, poured the milk, melted a bit of chocolate into it. I handed out mugs like it was a snowed-in Christmas.

Aliya blinked up at me. "Mommy… are we going home?"

I knelt beside her. "Soon, baby. When the storm's done. For now, we're safe. I promise."

Her small fingers wrapped around my wrist. "Did you beat the bad guy until he screamed like a granny?"

I looked toward the back room. Where Alec lay tied to a post, unconscious. Muzzled. Bleeding.

I nodded. "Yeah. I beat him."

When the kids finally began to fall asleep, curled together on thick fur rugs near the fire, I returned to the vault.

Behind a second hidden panel, I unlocked the safe.

It was still there.

The gold bars from Spain, stacked like bricks of justice, gleamed beneath the emergency lights. Even untouched, they shimmered with the kind of weight that didn't just buy homes—it bought governments.

Alec, the idiot, never even realized. He stole my companies. My name. My face.

But not my legacy.

Beside the bars, a Tupperware container full of diamonds. No case. No velvet. Just plastic and greed-proof locks.

All of it mine. All of it ours now.

Even without the empire, I was still a billionaire.

Still Catherine. Still Leon.

And still dangerous.

I sat down at the desk in the corner of the safe, a rusted chair I once used to draft emergency plans during war time. With the radio booster still working, I keyed in the code.

Static. Then a crackle.

"Joe," I said.

"Boss?" His voice came in slightly distorted, but strong.

"Storm's too heavy. No extraction tonight."

"I know. Blizzards locked us down at the tree line."

"There's a bunker here. Enough food for months. We're warm. Kids are safe."

"What about Alec?"

"Still breathing. Still bleeding."

Joe didn't ask more. He never did.

"You want me and the boys to come up?" he asked. "We'll bring coffee. Whiskey. Maybe play some cards."

I smiled for the first time in what felt like years.

"Yeah. Bring the old pack. Cabin's open."

"Copy that."

I returned upstairs and checked the bindings on Alec. He was half-conscious now, groaning behind the gag. His eyes opened and locked onto mine—filled with hate, with betrayal, with confusion.

"You never knew me," I whispered. "You thought you were playing chess with Catherine. But you never saw the third player."

I leaned close, my breath warm on his ear.

"You played with Leon. You died to Catherine. And now you rot beneath us both."

He growled something behind the gag. I stood and walked away, toward the fire, toward the sleeping children.

Outside, the storm howled harder. But inside, we were warm. Safe. Ready.

And tomorrow... when the sun rose and the winds died—

I would decide if Alec ever saw the sky again.

Two days later, the storm finally broke.

The snow melted slowly, like grief retreating. The thick drifts along the mountain pass thinned under sunlight that fought to warm the bones of the earth. Wind no longer howled like a grieving widow—it sighed, tired.

I loaded the kids into the backseat of the SUV.

Aliya was holding MJ's hand. Maya, ever the big sister now, wrapped Ivy's arms protectively around Jhing Jhing's precious daughter, who refused to let go of her unicorn. They were quiet—too quiet for children, but they had survived something no child should.

Behind me, Joe's convoy rumbled to life. Three black SUVs, snow-stained, windows tinted, guns locked and loaded. His men didn't speak much. But I saw it in their eyes—relief, respect, readiness for the next mission.

I called Mylene first.

She picked up on the second ring, voice already breaking. "Hello? Catherine?!"

"We got them," I said. "All of them. Safe. A little cold, a little tired... but safe."

There was a long pause. Then the sound of pure, raw sobbing.

"Oh my God—oh my God, Cathy—thank you… thank you…"

I heard the phone being passed. Jhing Jhing came on next, her voice already trembling with joy and disbelief.

"Is Ivy—"

"She's sleeping beside MJ right now," I said softly. "Aliya's holding her hand."

More crying. Softer this time. The kind of crying that only happens when the nightmare finally ends.

"We'll be there in a few hours," I promised.

"Drive safe," Jhing Jhing said. "We'll wait."

The sun was out when we reached the city. Slush gathered at the curbs. Life moved again—cars, dogs, people wrapped in coats and moving on with their little lives like the world hadn't almost collapsed in a storm.

Outside the apartment, Mylene and Jhing Jhing were already waiting. Arms outstretched. Eyes swollen from crying, lips trembling from holding it in.

The car hadn't even stopped when the back door flung open.

"Ivy!"
"MJ!"
"Aliya! Maya!"

It was chaos. Pure, emotional chaos. Mylene dropped to her knees, cradling my daughters like they'd been gone for years. Jhing Jhing wrapped her arms around MJ and Ivy, pressing her face into the girl's hair as if to memorize the scent. Tears. Kisses. Sobs. All at once. The kind of reunion you only see in warzones or soap operas.

And me?

I just stood there. Watching. Letting it all soak in.

Aliya turned her head and whispered, "Thank you, mommy."

That one little whisper unravelled me more than the gunshots, the storm, the blood.

That night, after the kids were all asleep in the master bedroom, we gathered in the living room. Me, Mylene, and Jhing.

We were exhausted. But not broken.

Mylene poured hot chocolate into three mismatched mugs. Jhing Jhing added a ridiculous number of marshmallows. I pulled the blanket tighter around my shoulders.

We didn't talk about the cabin.

We didn't mention Alec. The blood. The bruises. The storm. We knew if we did, someone would cry again—and we were done crying tonight.

So, we talked about normal things.

Shoes. The new winter collection from that overpriced boutique near downtown.

Jhing Jhing complained about her favourite highlighter going out of stock.

Mylene ranted about needing new jeans because her butt "got flatter from crying too much."

We laughed. Hard. The kind of laugh that stings the ribs.

"Tomorrow," Mylene said, raising her mug, "we will go to the salon."

"And get facials," Jhing Jhing added. "Our skin has suffered."

"And coffee," I smirked, sipping from my chipped pink Batman mug.

They both raised their mugs in agreement.

"No more crying," Jhing Jhing whispered.

"Not tonight," Mylene agreed. We hugged—tight, like survivors. Not as victims. But as women who came back from hell with their hearts still beating.

Tomorrow would be hair dye, new shoes, and overpriced lattes.

But tonight? Tonight was peace.

A month later, the headline came on a Monday morning. One of those cold, grey ones where even the coffee tastes tired. Mylene was flipping through the news on her tablet, half-reading aloud between bites of burnt toast and smears of peanut butter.

Then she paused.

Her voice dropped.

"Catherine..."

I didn't look up from tying Maya's shoelace. "What?" I asked, casually.

She turned the screen toward me.

"BREAKING: International Fugitive Alec Darrow Found Dead in Prison Cell – Suicide Suspected"

Dead. Alec. Gone. Like a whisper choked in a snowstorm.

I blinked.

"Finally," Jhing Jhing muttered from the hallway, holding Ivy's lunch bag.

I didn't say anything. I finished tying Maya's shoe, kissed her forehead, and sent the kids out the door with their snacks and scarves and laughter trailing behind them.

Only when the door clicked shut did I let the silence sit.

Mylene and Jhing Jhing watched me carefully.

I poured my coffee. Took a sip. And said flatly, "I'm not sad."

"No," Mylene said. "But you're not happy either."

"I'm not surprised," I answered.

Because the truth was—I couldn't kill him back at the cabin. Because part of Catherine wanted him to suffer. Alec just happened to kill himself before Leon could.

Whether it was guilt, fear, or the crushing weight of finally realizing he had lost everything—his name, his pride, his empire—I would never know.

And I didn't care to.

My empire returns. The world thought Alec had run everything. That he was the kingpin. The puppet master.

They were wrong. He was just the mask. *I was the venom.* And when he fell, I didn't let the empire rot. I took it back. Silently. Swiftly. And without mercy.

Not as Catherine. Not as Leon.

But as someone new.

BLACK WIDOW.

That was the name they whispered in *Monaco* boardrooms and *Dubai* lounges.

In the underground auctions of *Prague*, in the hacked channels of *Berlin*, in the moonlit syndicates of *Tokyo*. No one knew who I really was. A ghost. A legend. A power no one saw coming.

Except Joe. My loyal enforcer. My shadow in the dark. With his help—and the handful of allies who knew better than to cross me—I stitched together the empire like silk across old wounds. I didn't need to be loud. I didn't need to be seen. Power like mine was quiet. Elegant. Deadly.

Just like the camel toe of that silly maid.

Still, I lived in the same apartment. Three-bedroom, modern-industrial with the creaky stairs and a view of the city's beating heart. I could've moved. I could've bought a castle in the Alps or a villa in Mykonos.

But I didn't.

Because Maya, Aliya, and Jaya loved the playground next door.

Because Mylene would bang on my wall and say, "The pasta's burning again, you savage."

Because Jhing Jhing would show up barefoot in pyjamas with hair rollers and a bottle of rosé at 10 a.m. and say, "It's brunch somewhere."

Because sometimes the real treasure was just peace. So yes—I still went to the gym. Still did meal preps on Sundays. Still cursed the stairs every time the elevator broke down. And yes, I was no longer an oversized mom.

I was powerful. And I was free. But more than that—I was whole.

December came draped in lights and frost. The kids built snowmen with crooked smiles. Mylene made eggnog that nearly burned through the table. Jhing Jhing bought a karaoke machine, and by midnight, we were all screaming Mariah Carey like demons.

We gave gifts that didn't make sense—a pineapple-shaped handbag, glittered crocs, a mug that said "CEO of Chaos" *(mine, obviously)*.

The kids passed out under the new year's gift boxes.

And we—me, Mylene, and Jhing Jhing—sat on the couch, drinking expensive champagne, laughing over nothing, crying over even less. I looked around that night.

At the warm glow. At the safe sleep of children. At the two women beside me who had become my fortress.

And I felt something.

Not money. Not vengeance. Not the sweet sting of revenge or power. But something quieter. Something stronger.

Love. Not romantic. But the kind that builds an empire not from blood, but from bonds.

Somewhere, beneath the surface of that beautiful, normal life, the Black Widow still thrived.

My name was passed through encrypted servers.

A whisper here.

A threat there.

A deal made.

A hit called.

A country bought.

No one knew it was me.

The mom-jean boss of all badasses.

The End

Or not…

About the Author

C.Ellica

C.Ellica is the author of the English novel, Billionaire Accidental Wife, Loving the Alpha, The Merchant's Secret, Mr. Billionaire and I, A Taste of Temptation, The Chosen One, Desperate Thirst for Love which is available at some reading online platforms.

She is a mother of three and lives in the Philippines.

www.ingramcontent.com/pod-product-compliance
Lightning Source LLC
LaVergne TN
LVHW091622070526
838199LV00044B/900